WHO ARE YOU?

Donna

Donna Robbins

WESTBOW
P R E S S®
A DIVISION OF THOMAS NELSON
& ZONDERVAN

All Scripture is quoted from the Saint Joseph Edition of The New
American Bible, Catholic Book Publishing Co., New York, 1991

WestBow Press books may be ordered through
booksellers or by contacting:

WestBow Press
A Division of Thomas Nelson & Zondervan
1663 Liberty Drive
Bloomington, IN 47403
www.westbowpress.com
1 (866) 928-1240

ISBN: 978-1-4908-5415-1 (sc)

Library of Congress Control Number: 2014917942

Print information available on the last page.

WestBow Press rev. date: 12/2/2015

Contents

Donna: Good Morning!

Mrs. Sweetie: Who are you?

Donna: I am Donna.

Mrs. Sweetie: Who are you?

Donna: Who do you think I am?

Mrs. Sweetie: Donna.

Donna: That's right I'm Donna.

Mrs. Sweetie: I love you Donna.

Donna: I love you too Mrs. Sweetie.

Mrs. Sweetie: You call me Mrs. Sweetie, have I always been sweet?

Donna: Yes, you have always been sweet.

Mrs. Sweetie: Are we kidding each other?

Donna: No, we are not kidding each other.

Mrs. Sweetie: Are you my sister?

Donna: No, I am not your sister.

Mrs. Sweetie: Who are you then?

Donna: I'm your aide, Donna.

Mrs. Sweetie: I love you Donna.

Donna: I love you too Mrs. Sweetie.

Mrs. Sweetie: Who am I?

Donna: You are Mrs. Sweetie.

Mrs. Sweetie: I am?

Donna: Yes you are.

Mrs. Sweetie: Where is my father?

Donna: He has been deceased for many, many years. Mrs. Sweetie you are 94 years old.

Mrs. Sweetie: I am? I am really 94 years old?

Donna: Yes Mrs. Sweetie, you're really 94 years old.

Mrs. Sweetie: Who are you?

Donna: Who do you think I am?

Mrs. Sweetie: Donna.

Donna: That's right I'm Donna.

Mrs. Sweetie: I can't talk, I have no teeth.

Donna: You're doing a good job without them.

Mrs. Sweetie: No, I am not.

Donna: Okay, we will put your teeth in as soon as you get up.

Mrs. Sweetie: Who are you?

Donna: Who do you think I am?

Mrs. Sweetie: Donna.

Donna: Yes, that's right I am Donna.

Mrs. Sweetie: I love you Donna.

Donna: I love you too Mrs. Sweetie. It is time to get up.

Mrs. Sweetie: No! I want to stay in bed.

Donna: Mrs. Sweetie, it is ten thirty in the morning, don't you want some breakfast?

Mrs. Sweetie: Who are you?

Donna: Who do you think I am?

Mrs. Sweetie: Donna.

Donna: Yes, that's right. How about some breakfast now?

Mrs. Sweetie: Yes, I want some breakfast now. Who are you?

WHO ARE YOU?
DONNA!

Luke 11: 9, 10

9 And I tell you, ask and you will receive; seek and you will find; knock and the door will be opened to you. 10 For everyone who ask, receives; and the one who seeks, finds; and to the one who knocks, the door will be opened to you.

All Scripture is quoted from the Saint Joseph Edition of The Catholic Study Bible, New

American Bible, Oxford University Press, Inc, New York, 1990.

SIRACH 41: 12, 13
12 Have a care for your name, for it will stand by you better than precious treasures in the thousands; 13 The boon of life is for limited days, but a good name, for days without number.

Reputation is what men and women think of us; character is what God and angels know of us.- Thomas Paine

Thank you dear Heavenly Father, Son, and Holy Spirit for your love and gifts that You have given me through the years. Dear Lord I pray that the ones reading this book overlook any grammar errors and open their hearts to accept what You reveal to them through the pages of this book.

Romans 11:29, For the gifts and the call of God are irrevocable.

I am especially grateful for my husband John and our three children, Johnnie, Heather, and Sarah for having faith and patience in me that impelled this book forward after I had given up. Your sincere desire to hear these stories each night before bedtime provided the encouragement to put those spoken words onto paper for others to read. These stories also transcended into life lessons for our family as we studied the word of God together that provided encouragement when faced with battles that challenged our Godly beliefs as we strived to walk daily with Jehovah.

1 Peter 4:10 As each one has received a gift, use it to serve one another as good stewards of God's varied grace.

God has blessed our family over the years with three children and four beautiful grandchildren, Hunter, Elizabeth, Ayden, Faith, and four in Heaven waiting for their Nana. Never forget how important your family truly is.

My son always said, "My love for you blooms like a dessert flower." – Johnnie Phipps.

In order for the dessert wild flowers to bloom, many components are involved in orchestrating that bloom such as the sun, water, and temperature. Families are like the dessert wildflowers, they also need components like love, understanding, compassion, truth, and God in order to blossom. The Holy Family can be a paradigm for all families regardless of their beliefs. Human families are broken and imperfective in a world full of evil. When we arrive in heaven to live with our Lord, Jesus Christ, only then will we experience perfect love. Families today are photoshopped for perfectionism but in reality, families are not thriving because not all the components are coming together. Some families never flourish, while others seem to be prospering in difficult seasons where as other families gain strength as they expand. Are any of these components missing from your family?

Ephesians 3: 14-21

14 For this reason I kneel before the Father, 15 from whom every family in heaven and on earth is named, 16 that he may grant you in accord with the riches of his glory to be strengthened with power through his Spirit in the inner self, 17 and that Christ may dwell in your hearts through faith; that you, rooted and grounded in love, 18 may have strength to comprehend with all the holy ones what is the breadth and length and height and depth, 19 and to know the love of Christ that surpasses knowledge, so that you may be filled with all the fullness of God. 20 Now to him who is able to accomplish far more than all we ask or imagine, by the power at work within us, 21 to him be glory in the church and in Christ Jesus to all generations, forever and ever. Amen.

Introduction

My husband, John proclaims that I have a knack for asking questions that are hard to answer, especially concerning matters of the heart (feelings) but in reality, I don't. People who depend on others for help with everyday tasks are the ones who truly ask the hardest question, "Who are you?"

I am Donna, as you may have guessed that was a Certified Nursing Assistant (CNA) and a Home Health Care Aide (HHA) for 15 years. The goal of this book is to help you realize how individuals in the health care field are dedicated to helping those you love or maybe even you in the future. Most of all, I hope this book inspires human beings to walk closer to God. Please say a prayer for a health care worker or give a health care worker a small ray of hope to keep going through a word of encouragement. What they do for others is worth it every day.

Have you heard of elder abuse or mistreatment of the elderly by HHA's and/or CNA's? Did you form an opinion about that health care provider? After you read this book maybe you will understand our role in the health care field. Within the pages of this book, the stories will escort you through the lives of human beings that we care for. As in every profession, there are those who give the rest a bad name, but that doesn't represent all of us. After all, aren't we all human beings?

Proverbs 22: 1, 2

1 A good name is more desirable than great riches, and high esteem, than gold and silver. 2 Rich and poor have a common bond: the LORD is the maker of them all.

What's in a name?

"That which we call a rose by any other name would smell as sweet." -William Shakespeare

As you go through your everyday tasks or job duties think about what it means to care for another person. Then ask yourself what it must be like to care for another human being and then ask a CNA/HHA. If you have time to listen to them, I really mean if you make time to listen to their narrative it will evoke emotions of anger, make you laugh or cry, sadden your spirit or fill you with an abundance of emotions including joy. These stories are life lessons that can change your heart about human beings in general if you decide to truly listen.

I am grateful for the human beings that have touched my life through my job as a CNA/HHA as they allowed me into their lives to learn valuable lessons concerning human behavior. Hope you enjoy these true stories that demonstrate just how much we need each other, even when we don't realize that we do. The stories that you are about to read are all true but the names have been changed to protect their identity.

CHAPTER 1

Who Are You?

Many of us when asked this question, who are you, will respond with our name, but the elderly that I cared for were questioning the authenticity of the care giver, me. The realism for this conclusion began in 1985, that's when I decided to become a certified nursing assistant (CNA). The primary factor governing this decision was money. I did not know that in this change of career to a CNA that I, Donna would discover my true calling as I continued my spiritual journey that would uncover the things that would change my heart forever about other human beings.

Colossians 3:12-17
12 Put on then, as God's chosen ones, holy and beloved, heartfelt compassion, kindness, humility, gentleness, and patience, 13 bearing with one another and forgiving one another,

if one has a grievance against another; as the Lord has forgiven you, so must you also do. 14 And over all these put on love, that is, the bond of perfection. 15 And let the peace of Christ control your hearts, the peace into which you were also called in one body. And be thankful. 16 Let the word of Christ dwell in you richly, as in all wisdom you teach and admonish one another, singing psalms, hymns, and spiritual songs with gratitude in your hearts to God. 17 And whatever you do, in word or in deed, do everything in the name of the Lord Jesus, giving thanks to God, the Father through him.

Stop, imagine yourself sitting in your favorite chair as you hear a knock at your door. You answer the door and a stranger announces that he/she are there to help you with your personal care and walks through your front door. Now, imagine that this stranger who just entered your home is placing their hands on your body in broad daylight. What are your thoughts at this moment as you realize that a stranger is going to unclothe you and place their hands somewhere on your body? Use the following space to write down any thoughts or feelings that have come to your mind.

_____

_____

_____

_____

_____

_____

In 1985, the cost for a thirty-five hour course titled Certified Nursing Assistant (CNA) was thirty dollars. When reflecting back upon the decision to become a CNA, it seems anomalous that the cost of Judas betraying Jesus Christ was also thirty pieces of silver. For my thirty dollars, I received a big blue book that described how to use proper body mechanics.

1st Timothy 4:8 for, while physical training is of limited value, devotion is valuable in every respect, since it holds a promise of life both for the present and for the future.

Okay this sounded easy enough, even though I didn't know anything about garages; yes, this was just how foreign this new career was to me at the time. Did I lose you with this last sentence about garages? If your answer was yes, then you understand just how Greek it was to me also at that time. Later I learned where my true strength would come from, God. This big blue book did not prepare anyone that took the CNA class for tough issues concerning human beings. These issues became lessons in a classroom that I call the "metamorphosis of real life" that changed the value I placed on human beings. This progression retrained my heart while I worked with human beings for the next 14 years. During this change, I betrayed Jesus Christ many, many times before surrendering myself to God's will and not my own. How little did I know or realize then how I would mature spiritually by working with human beings that would produce the greatest fortune and rewards for a small sum of thirty dollars that seemed like such a large sum of money at that time in my life.

Caregivers have many boundaries to conquer, but once conquered, they realize that the periphery of their feelings masquerades their inner feelings that connect their mind, body, and soul.

Especially when dealing with issues such as religion, race, mental and physical challenges, cleanliness, body weight, death, friendship, and I almost forgot, dogs. Caregivers and clients have to confront their feelings regarding these issues in order to work together, but the effects will last for many years afterwards. The misconceptions of reality are about to become real. Buckle your seat belt! You are going to experience the alterations of metamorphosis due to real life classroom experiences as an HHA/CNA. Safety checks; are your seatbelts (hearts) on and buckled (opened)? There are things you're going to realize about your own self as you read this book. Some of these issues just might change your heart or help you to heal a hurt, maybe yours, or someone else's. How many of us really like change or should I ask how many of us want to change, even when it is for the better. Let's go a little deeper, do you become uncomfortable or feel your insides quiver just at the mention of these issues that I mentioned earlier? If you could change one thing about yourself, what would that be? Write it down. Don't forget to be completely honest with yourself. The child within us often forgets until reminded by our adult reasoning.

_____

_____

_____

_____

1st Corinthians 13: 11-12
11 When I was a child, I used to talk as a child, think as a child, reason as a child; when I became a man, I put aside childish things. 12 At present we see indistinctly, as in a mirror, but then face to face. At present I know partially; then I shall know fully, as I am fully known.

The next twelve chapters will provide some resolution to the question that the elderly I worked with asked of me, 'who you are'. I will rephrase this question to reflect what the elderly may be asking, "who is this caregiver, Donna, can I trust her?" Take a moment to reflect upon these questions and then ask yourself, who am I and can I be trusted? Then if you feel brave enough ask someone else, who do you think I am.

WHO AM I

By: Sarah Robbins

I am a very intelligent young girl
Who has a mind of her own
Can I change the world that I live in

I am only one person
In this world
I believe I can make a difference

First
I must change myself
I am whom I want and choose to be
By God's design

Ephesians 5: 20 giving thanks always and for everything in the name of our Lord Jesus Christ to God the Father.

CHAPTER 2

A Look Behind the Mask

Remember that little exercise in chapter one where I asked you to jot down your feelings about a stranger touching your body? Now, stop for a few minutes and think about being a CNA. You paid your thirty dollars, took the course, passed the test and now you're an aide. You have arrived at your first case. You review the list of supplies that your supervisor told you to take with you to this case when you spoke to her on the phone. You approach the house and knock on the door; a very skinny man answers the door that looks as if he just awakened from a forty year nap. His body odor penetrates the entrance way, you realize that you are stepping backwards. You're fighting hard not to cover your mouth and nose with your hand as your stomach becomes queasy. At the same time, you question if your eyes are deceiving you as you wonder if this is man or animal, his face completely covered by hair that goes down almost to his waist. You are struggling to find his eyes when suddenly you see two dark, round marbles set deeply within a forest of eyebrows. Then you realize that every inch of his exposed body is covered with a thick mass of hair. Something inside of you says run as you are deciding whether or not to go through that door. What thoughts are you thinking? Write them down.

_____

_____

_____

_____

_____

_____

Okay, remember those issues I previously mentioned, well, this is one of those issues. His body odor is turning your stomach and his outer appearance makes you feel very uncomfortable with all his hair. All this combined makes your own skin crawl knowing that you will have to touch him in order to help with his personal care since he is in a wheelchair. Your thoughts are interrupted as this hostile voice breaks the silence; "You're five minutes late! Don't you know what time it is? I've already called that company you work for to let them know that you're late."

You look at your wrist watch and you are five minutes early. You step through the door and Mr. Wolf's coo, coo clock is going coo, coo, coo, coo. You find yourself saying to Mr. Wolf, "but sir I have five minutes till eight and your coo, coo clock is still coo, cooing for eight o'clock and you claim I'm five minutes late." Mr. Wolf starts to reply, but the coo, coo clock has not reached the eight coo, coo yet and drowns out his response. "So what if I have bad eyesight too."

Okay, so you were dreaming that this client would be a little old grandfather who thought you were little red riding hood coming to visit. You misplaced the wolf in the story, that's all. You huff and puff under your breath as your thoughts are working overtime to compensate for not being able to verbalize your thoughts. You don't remember reading anything in that blue book that prepared a person for this. Your thoughts are getting the best of you. You know that you have to try to rationalize this client's behavior and yours since the supervisor reminded you before coming to this case that the client has rights; that should have been a clue that you were walking into troubled water or the forest. Your mind keeps conveying the thought over and over that you have rights too when Mr. Wolf's words drown out your thoughts. You hear a voice that sounds so furious, "Well, are you going to stand there all day? Close the door, the air-conditioner is running. Would you like to pay my bill?" "No" I replied abruptly. Then he yelled to close the door as he rolled into the kitchen.

You wish that Mr. Wolf would see the steam that was coming from the back of your neck. You feel your forehead and behind to see if someone placed a sticker there that reads you're a fool or kick me as you close the door. You then place your belongings in a chair by the door, which brought on his next outburst, "Don't put your things in my chair. Don't they teach you girls anything? Don't you know how to ask? Do you do that at your home?"

"Which question do you want answered first or do I just summarize them all for you?" OOPS, did you just actually say that to Mr. Wolf, yes you did. The slip of your tongue mystified you, but Mr. Wolf's next words bewildered you as he announced with boldness, "So you are a smart ass too I see!" His comment makes you question your own actions. Are you being as rude as Mr. Wolf? Do you want to explain this to your supervisor? Have you ever opened your mouth only to find that your shoe size doesn't fit so well? You begin to explain how sorry you are for upsetting him, "Sir, I did not mean it the way that it sounded. I have upset you so I will call the office and tell them to send another aide." Mr. Wolf began to stutter as he said in a very low, soft growl, "No, don't do that. It will take them all day to get someone else out here. They are as bad as the people they send."

I do not know how you would react to Mr. Wolf, but this was my reaction to him and I was amazed at my own words, "I'm sorry we make you feel that way. I didn't mean to upset you. I'll try very hard to get here tomorrow on time. I will even set my wrist watch by your coo, coo clock so that I know I will be here by your time." I cannot believe this, I'm trying to be polite under these circumstances, and all he can say to me is, "Don't get here too early. I don't want to get up one minute earlier than I have to." All right you nasty, hairy little old man, if you only knew what I wanted to do to you, but my feelings went numb as he interrupted a perfectly bad thought with, "Don't think too hard young lady, you'll catch your brains on fire."

What is this with this man? This situation had turned into a challenge; is this man capable of reading my thoughts. I really needed to get a grip on this conversation and get out from behind the eight ball. What excuse could I use to leave, and then suddenly he changed the mood with his next words. "I like to look into people's faces. You can pretty much tell what they are thinking by watching the movement of their bottom jaw. That's why I wear this hair on my face. If I didn't have my beard I couldn't be this mean, because you would see me smiling at you right now."

One moment of silence can seem like an eternity. Just a simple why, was my only response. "Close your mouth young lady before something flies into it." I could only stare at him. Again, he responded, "Would you like for me to repeat what I just said?" He was just as shocked as I was with my response. "Hello Mr. Wolf, I'm Donna, your aide for today. How are you sir?" I held out my hand and he shook it as he gave me a tender squeeze and turned quickly wiping away a tear. For the first time since I arrived, I looked straight into his eyes.

Philippians 1:20 My eager expectation and hope is that I shall not be put to shame in any way, but that with all boldness, now as always, Christ will be magnified in my body, whether by life or death.

Do human beings really realize what they say or that how they say it truly impacts another human being when they greet them for the first time? Would this have happened if I had taken the time to really look at him when I arrived? I saw his outer appearance first and never greeted the human being behind the mask. I couldn't wait to tell him he was wrong about the jaw, but in fact, it was the eyes that let you see how much a person could be hurting. This would have to wait for another day. I wanted to cherish this moment that we just shared. In fact that day never came. I learned a lesson that day regarding how we actually should greet other human beings.

Baruch 3:12-15
12 You have forsaken the fountain of wisdom! 13 Had you walked in the way of God, you would have dwelt in enduring peace. 14 Learn where prudence is, where strength, where understanding; That you may know also where

are length of days, and life, where light of the eyes, and peace 15 Who has found the place of wisdom, who has entered into her treasuries?

Chinese fortune cookie: What is the distance between the eyes and the soul?

A Different Love

By: Donna Robbins

Love
One that's willing to bend
Like the big trees swaying in the wind

Love of oneself
Enough to share to all mankind

A different love
Than we have ever known

A willingness
From within to love each other's faults
More than the things, that pleases us most

Donna Robbins

I'm talking of a different love
A different feeling
That when we reach out
We can feel peace with each other

A different love
Created in the heart
By
A love of Jesus
To a friend
Here upon this earth

CHAPTER 3

What Issues?

You're off to another case. A man greets you at the front door, but he is not your client. Did you look into his eyes as you greeted him? He invites you in with a gracious smile and introduces you to the woman of the house, his wife, Mrs. Ice-Icicle. She is your next learning assignment. She is a statue of ice, frozen deep within a cavern of illness, unwinding deeper and deeper into darkness; standing by her side still stood her husband, whose smile was now a scream of agony and torture that appeared upon his face.

Your eyes meet Mrs. Ice-Icicle's when a feeling of cold runs down your spine that you can't explain. Your voice quivered as you pronounced your name to Mrs. Ice-Icicle. Remember when I said that you realize after the moment that you did not do or say the correct thing. Well, you just forgot to extend your hand towards her as you greeted her for the first time; funny how fear will seize your emotions and cripple you. You feel as if you are surrounded by a fog when you hear her penetrating words, "You may put your things over there on the chair by the door. Then you can wash the windows outside today. My husband has the hose-pipe and cleaning supplies ready for you outside the back door."

How would you tell Mrs. Ice-Icicle that you are a CNA and that you are there to help with her personal care not to fulfill the position of window washer?

_____

_____

_____

_____

_____

I summoned my voice from the icy fog surrounding us, "Mrs. Ice-Icicle, sorry but I am not here to do your windows." Mrs. Ice-Icicle's smile turns awkward revealing hoarfrost upon her frozen lips. "There are some cleaning supplies under the kitchen sink that you can use to clean the air vents then." As she finished saying these words, I realized that I had followed the direction of her hand that was pointing upwards. I precisely ended this madness. Sorry to say that Mrs. Ice-Icicle did not like to hear that I could not clean her air vents and that I was there to help her with her personal care. Mrs. Ice-Icicle remained calm but cold as an ice cube while taking much delight in telling me that she had already bathed with her husband's help earlier that morning and that she would prefer that I would at least polish her silverware before I left.

The simplest words spoken brought forth the greatest storm when I informed Mrs. Ice-Icicle that I was not there to polish her silverware and that it would be best if I called the office to let them talk to her about why I was there. The storm raged into full motion and I found myself directly in the eye of the storm as she launched her words towards me, "Never mind, just leave."

Knowing that I had to have her sign my paperwork I sat down at the dining room table to complete it. Just as my bottom touched her chair, my 115 pound body jumped up very fast. I couldn't believe what I was seeing or hearing from Mrs. Ice-Icicle. She was jumping up and down screaming, "Get off of my chair now. You are too heavy. You will break my chair. Get out of my house now!"

I gathered my paperwork together and asked her to sign it and she refused. With only inches between us, she tossed daggers of ice words. I panicked and gathered my belongings then headed towards the door. As I opened the door I felt her hand greet the middle of my back as she began pushing me out the door, I wasn't moving fast enough for her. I felt the wind from the door as she slammed it shut behind me. I went to the nearest payphone to call the office to let them know what had just happened and that she refused to sign any paperwork. As I sat there thinking about what had taken place I glimpsed through the blue book and found nothing about mental health issues. Clearly, I needed some training in this area.

Is it okay to have feelings that are judgmental as long as you don't let those feelings cloud your judgment? Are your feelings different than the ones at the beginning of chapter one?

Yes _____ No _____

Take a moment to reflect on those differences and write them down. Are your feelings from the heart? If they are then compare them to the other thoughts that you have written down.

_____

_____

_____

_____

_____

_____

Donna Robbins

What was the difference?

_____

_____

_____

_____

Every day events that occur in your life are training tools for your spiritual walk. When you choose not to use what you learned from those events then you begin to dry up spiritually and if you refuse to treat others as God instructs us to treat his human beings then you become a slave to un-forgiveness. Freedom, free indeed, yes God gives you free choice to serve and obey his plan regarding treatment of others. If you chose not to obey God, then don't complain when you no longer experience any joy and blessings stop coming your way, or that you find yourself being treated the way that you have treated others.

Philippians 2:3-5
3 Do nothing out of selfishness or out of vainglory; rather, humbly regard others as more

important than yourselves, 4 each looking out not for his own interest, but [also] everyone for those of others. 5 Have among yourselves the same attitude that is also yours in Christ Jesus.

The mind can be as breathtaking as the view of Niagara Falls, the Grand Canyon, or newly fallen snow. They all are wonders that show the beauty of God's handy work, just like the mind when he created man in his image.

Genesis 1: 27, 28
God created man in his image; in the divine image he created him; male and female he created them. 28 God blessed them, saying: "Be fertile and multiply; fill the earth and subdue it. Have dominion over the fish of the sea, the birds of the air, and all the living things that move on the earth."

Imagine you are sitting in your favorite chair enjoying a cup of tea after your usual Saturday afternoon visit with your two year old grandson when you see the toys that seem to be smiling as they still lay there on the floor in front of you. Suddenly there is a weird feeling in your head. It is different and strange, then nothing but pain. The room begins spinning and you feel yourself losing body control as you try to stand. You can't stand, everything's blurred, lights out.

A light unexpectedly appears. You awake in a room that is not your own. It takes effort for you to focus. Things are still blurry. The light is very bright as it shines in your eyes. You tell the light to stop. You listen. You can't hear your words. You know that you are moving your lips. Words, where are they? Where is the sound of water, like a brook coming from? In your mind you ask yourself, where am I. You speak again but still no words do you hear. You listen more closely then you realize it is not water that you hear but a gargling sound. It is coming from you. A tear forms, your first realization that something is terribly wrong with you.

You raise your hand to push the light away. Where is your hand? You reach over your body with your other hand and find your missing hand. Can you trust your senses? Your fingers tell your brain that the hand is still there. The skin feels cold, dead. What a strange sensation. You try to move your foot. It is heavy. You realize that the right side of your body is not working. Over the next few days the doctor confirms, your body is unresponsive. You are trapped in own body. You can no longer speak, stand, go to the bathroom, or feed yourself. Only memories left. You realize you are useless. You have had a stroke.

Six months later, you are unenthusiastic due to the dreadful task of trying to regain your physical and mental processes. You realize the words that came so easy while teaching your grandson his ABC's are very difficult now that you have to learn to speak them again. Your daughter and speech therapist persistently try to teach you how to speak and to write your name. Your grandson and physical therapist diligently try to teach you to walk and feed yourself again. These activities have taken over your daily life that completely consume every ounce of energy and strength you can muster. You no longer enjoy long walks on the beach, reading a book, or singing in the choir. You experience days of gloom with very little sunshine. Two things nag at your heart constantly. The first, your heart breaks every time your grandson asks you to play with him. He doesn't understand the words you say or why you won't play with him. He becomes frustrated with you and runs to his mother crying. The second hurts worse than the first. Your family members talk about you behind your back. They think that you can't understand them. They do not include you in their adult conversations. They talk to you like you are a baby. The worst, they never look into your eyes.

Another six months pass. Your family members are so happy. You just wrote your name again. Your daughter wants to frame it. You have not mastered complete sentences again so you verbalize words that claim it is chicken scratch. The family praises you. You weep inside. They remind you of how far you have come in the last six months and the progress you made, and how lucky you are to still be alive. The stroke paralyzed your body not your memories; they are all that you have left of the life you had. No one has to remind you of how far your life has brought you. How do you get them to understand that you are dealing with this stroke too the best way that you can?

Your heart whispers to them, I love you, but it longs for release. Your aide hears your cries. How does she seem to hear when others don't? She picks up on things more than you want her to; about the one thing that you don't want anyone to know. She hears that little something in your voice that you cannot hide any longer. Your aide voices a response to the feelings that you have wanted to scream out loud for months, "Mrs. Grandma you can't give up." Your eyes meet and you both know the thought that has lingered for months, you just want to die. Both did not know how quickly that wish for death would come. In twenty-four hours another stroke had completely undone all the hard work that was accomplished that last year. Death came quickly after her third stroke; her wish granted.

Death takes your friend. You were not there to hold her hand or say good bye; a new issue, guilt. Before this issue can grip your heart and let you feel the pain, you have a new client. As months pass, you realize the importance of not letting this issue, guilt, take any foothold in your life since it serves no purpose to help you heal or forget.

Book of Wisdom 1: 12-15
12 Court not death by your erring way of life, nor draw to yourselves destruction by the works of your hands. 13 Because God did not make death, nor does he rejoice in the destruction of the living. 14 For he fashioned all things that they might have being; and the creatures of the world are wholesome, And there is not a destructive drug among them nor any domain of the neither world on earth, 15 For justice is undying.

After you dry your tears I will make you laugh. You arrive at your client's home and knock on the door. You are standing there waiting for your client to answer when you notice how beautiful this front door once was. The weather and lack of care had taken its toll upon this door as it hung in its rusty frame. Its color goes with the outside theme; it is a beautiful barnyard red. It is almost Christmas and you are thinking how fitting the color of the door is at this time of the year. You notice a piece of what use to be a wreath hanging on the door. Your thoughts begin to imagine what this place could look like with your special touch. The door swings open and you prepare to greet your client standing there in the doorway when he comes into full view; standing there in front of you was a little old man with cheeks as red as cherries. You wonder how red your face is at this "Kodak" moment. Should you run or laugh. You quickly regain your composure and introduce yourself. "Hello, I'm Donna, your aide. Are you Mr. Santa Clause?

You stand there waiting for his reply, "Yes." Then you walk quickly by your client standing in front of you wearing nothing but a red and white Santa hat and black boots. He closes the door, walks over to his chair, and sits down. What happened over the next couple of hours I will leave to each one's own illusions? I will add that my curiosity was satisfied to see if his belly really did shake like jelly. Oh, come on and laugh.

Update: About a week later, a highway patrolman found Mr. Santa Clause in another state. He did not know who he was or where he lived. Mr. Santa Clause didn't have ID with him due to his attire, only a red and white Santa hat and black boots. The patrolman had the license plates traced; they revoked his driver's licenses. The police detained him overnight in the other state and released him the next day to his family. They took away his car/sled.

On New Year's Eve, following this incident Mr. Santa Clause gave some of his neighbors an unexpected fright, while others laughed until daylight as they watched Mr. Santa Clause walking down the street singing. Yes, he was still wearing his favorite suit, only a red and white hat and matching black boots.

Job 1: 21 and said, "Naked I came forth from my mother's womb, and naked shall I go back again. The LORD gave and the LORD has taken away; blessed be the name of the LORD!"

There is just one question that I will ask you. What makes a person pretend that they are never going to be old and lose their mind? It is amazing that just the mention of old age brings out the fear that we may become a Santa Clause or Mrs. Clause too.

Matthew 18:1-5
1 At that time the disciples approached Jesus and said, "Who is the greatest in the kingdom of heaven?" 2 He called a child over, placed it in their midst, 3 and said, "Amen, I say to you, unless you turn and become like children,

you will not enter the kingdom of heaven. 4 Whoever humbles himself like this child is the greatest in the kingdom of heaven. 5 And whoever receives one child such as this in my name receives me.

The Unthinkable Child

By: Donna Robbins

As I return to my childhood from old age
And become your child
Will you choose not to see the good within my heart

When you conceive that, my emotions don't match yours

Will you try to conquer them

This child I will become
Will you see me as having no real value
Even though you have always been my world

Others will see me empty of love
If you choose not to refill me with your love
I loved you my child with all my heart

I will feel worthless
If you chose to ignore what I can still offer
To you and my grandchildren

Impossible you say
Well then retrain me with love
Do you not realize
I need more of your time
Than you are willing to give

Remember when I put all things aside for you

Sometimes you call me a monster or other names
Is that what I am to you
I know I can never be your parent again as in
the past
But I am still your parent
only different

You voice that you wish you could escape
From having to care for me
So do I
Maybe in another home
My life would be easier

I dream too

When I bring you my feelings of loneliness
You say I'm preposterous
At least I am honest, why aren't you

A vain child you say I am becoming
But do you realize
I still compromise for you
I am equally hopeless of my surroundings
Just as you are
Unimaginable in your mind
Of what I could still offer or be again
A place where you will visit one day
As I

The Book of Wisdom 7: 1-6

1 I too am a mortal man, the same as all the rest, and a descendant of the first man formed of earth. And in my mother's womb I was molded into flesh in a ten-months' period—body and blood, from the seed of man, and the pleasure that accompanies marriage. 3 And I too, when born, inhaled the common air, and fell upon the kindred earth; wailing, I uttered that first sound common to all. 4 In swaddling clothes and with constant care I was nurtured. 5 For no king has any different origin or birth, 6 but one is the entry into life for all; and in one same way they leave it.

Mr. Santa Clause must have been cold those nights, but he was singing and having fun enjoying his old age. As each of us age in the future, can we say that we will not be a Mr. or Mrs. Santa Clause? I just hope that I am happy if I experience this stage of life and live in a warm climate.

Sirach 37: 16-25

16 A word is the source of every deed; a thought, of every act. 17 The root of all conduct is the mind; four branches it shouts forth: 18 Good and evil, death and life, their absolute mistress is the tongue. 19 A man may be wise and benefit many, yet be of no use to himself. 20 Though a man may be wise, if his words are rejected he will be deprived of all enjoyment. 21 When a man is wise to his own advantage, the fruits of his knowledge are seen in his own person; 22 When a man is wise to his people's advantage, the fruits of his knowledge are enduring: 23 Limited are the days of one man's life, but the life of Israel is days without number. 24 One wise for himself has full enjoyment, and all who see him praise him; 25 One wise for his people wins a heritage of glory, and his name endures forever.

CHAPTER 4

Grace

This lady was dependent on the use of a wheelchair due to debilitating effects from a stroke. My children's observation of her wheelchair was that it was their chariot. In the eyes of my children, it didn't matter that she could not get out of bed or stand without help, or that she was not able to use the bathroom or bath without help. It did not matter to the children that one side of her mouth sagged or drooled like them. Her paralyzed body from the stroke made her no different or scarier than any other adult that didn't ride in a chariot in my children's eyes.

In the living world of human beings, my children saw a person with a disability as a kind, loving human being who shared laughter, friendship, and love with them. They learned at a very early age that human beings with a disability are loving and not someone they have to be afraid of. One memory that proved this took place at a grocery store. Another human being in a wheelchair, not our lady, approached my girls, age's two and three in one of the grocery store aisles and before I could stop them they were already climbing on her wheelchair as the youngest one had managed to climb onto this strangers' lap. The look upon this stranger's face as one child stood on the footrest of the wheelchair and the other child in her lap was priceless. This stranger was confused but pleased. I quickly started explaining how the children rode on the wheelchair with the lady that I took care of as I managed to get them off her. I quickly learned that adults could benefit from seeing the world through the eyes of a child. This stranger now realized that her wheelchair was a chariot. She seemed to be in a happier mood as she rolled out of sight.

Upon the lap they would sit
Of a beautiful lady
All of them going on a trip

With wheels for legs and mama behind
Pushing them around all the time

Ephesians 4:11-16
And he gave some as apostles, others as prophets, others as evangelists, others as pastors and teachers, 12 to equip the holy ones for the work of ministry, for building up the body of Christ, 13 until we all attain to the unity of faith and knowledge of the Son of God, to mature manhood, to the extent of the full stature of Christ, 14 so that we may no longer be infants, tossed by waves and swept along by every wind of teaching arising from human trickery, from their cunning in the interests of deceitful scheming. 15 Rather, living the truth in love, we should grow in every way into him who is the head, Christ, 16 from whom the whole body, joined and held together by every supporting ligament, with the proper functioning of each part, brings about the body's growth and builds itself up in love.

My children and I were blessed beyond what mankind measures. Some humans view growing up around the elderly as boring. My children to this day have no problem being with an older person, giving them a hug or holding their hand. I allowed the elderly to touch the life of my children as often as possible. Due to both sets of maternal grandparents not living in the same state, we adopted several older people as grandparents in our neighborhood. I pray that they never lose the ability to feel comfortable around the best history books that mankind will ever possess, our elders.

Proverbs 4: 1-9

Wisdom: the Supreme Guide of Men

1 Hear, O children, a father's instruction, be attentive, that you may gain understanding! 2 Yes, excellent advise I give you; my teaching do not forsake, 3 When I was my father's child, frail, yet the darling of my mother, 4 He taught me, and said to me: "Let your heart hold fast my words: keep my commands, that you may live! 5 "Get wisdom, get understanding! Do not forget or turn aside from the words I utter. 6 Forsake her not, and she will preserve you; love her,

and she will safeguard you; 7 The beginning of wisdom is: get wisdom; at the cost of all you have, get understanding. 8 Extol her, and she will exalt you; she will bring you honors if you embrace her; 9 She will put on your head a graceful diadem; a glorious crown will she bestow on you."

The greatest malady this nation will encounter will be to ignore our elders. What we are doing in the name of humanity when society neglects to harvest the benefits that the young and old together produce? The declining interaction between the young and old will result in family bonds from our generation to future generations to be broken. The elderly are the fine sand needed to create the mortar that holds all of society together. Without young and old united, we are doomed to fall apart as a civilization.

Our Grandparents

By Donna Robbins

GRANDMOTHER
Out of you we came
Look at our eyes
How they glow like yours
Our heart that cares like yours
Our hands as they imitate yours
Your compassion when we are ill
Your persistence when it is something we don't
want to do
Never the less
We get our good looks from you

GRANDFATHER
Out of you came
Our wisdom to accomplish the impossible
Your strength to carry our plans through
Your capability to love
The intelligence to endure
And the seeds of trust we must sow as you

So from both of you we got
The most important parts
As we thrust forth in our search of life
We carry on the gifts that you passed into
US

Leviticus 19: 32 "Stand up in the presence of the aged, and show respect for the old; thus shall you fear your God. I am the LORD.

Miss. Grace always displayed calmness. You could sit in her presence and feel the power and peace that came from her prayers while she prayed the Rosary. This was my first introduction to the Rosary and the blessings that it contains through faith. I will always remember the peace that flowed from her as she helped me to see things with a different mindset concerning religions. She modeled a contentment of peace as she walked with God in the Catholic faith just as I had seen my own mother, grandmother, and great-grandmother in their Baptist faith.

Miss. Grace loved to hear the poems that I wrote and insisted on hearing something each day. I was standing on her front porch after praying with her one day when the poem Foreign Winter was whispered into existence, which is in another chapter. Then one day I read her a poem that I had written just for her, Beauty of Grace. From that day forward, she requested that I read her poem daily until she left this earth.

BEAUTY OF GRACE

By: Donna Robbins

The name only adores the beauty held within
Each fine line bears a decade of faith
Each movement of limbs
Still with amazement of some to wonder on

Age of Grace is a miracle itself
A gift created by God
Held sacred till the end

Each white hair
Each wrinkle of the skin made from time
For the heavens, earth, and angels to rejoice
For no man can duplicate the beauty of Grace

So as we absorb the beauty
That comes from within
We long to endure
Each smile held dear
Each look of wisdom held near
To keep alive
What has inspired through the years

CHAPTER 5

Me, a Girl Named Sue

This was my first encounter with my secret sister. Her name was Sue; my middle name too. She was my client, but in my mind, she could have been me because we shared so many of the same traits. This stranger tap danced around the idea that she was me too from the moment that we met. Sue kept pointing to me and repeating, "Me? Me? Me?" It was as if she and I were discovering layer by layer a non-genealogical closeness as our spirits aroused each other. Over time, I realized that we had many things in common: height, weight, color of hair, and very similar tastes in food, clothes, and decorations. She seemed more than an acquaintance and I believe she felt the same. This is why I named her Sue, after myself.

Sue was my first actual client with a diagnosis of Alzheimer's. Her personas came across as being a very delightful person, especially if her husband was around. Both Sue and her husband were in their late eighties. The love that they once shared was now as fragile as their age. Sue's husband refused to put her into a nursing home. I soon learned that Sue's husband was a stranger in their house just as much as the other aides and I. The first observation that her husband was a stranger occurred one evening shortly after I started working there. I had prepared a meal for the both of them since it was just as easy to cook for two as one. I served them their meal, started to turn to the sink when out of the corner of my eye I caught Sue aiming her fork at her husband. Before I could stop her from throwing the fork, it hit her husband directly on the forehead. Sue started screaming, "Get out, get out." He quietly picked up his plate and went into the dining room to eat. I followed him to see if he was injured. He informed me that he was okay and this was usual behavior for her to throw things at him because sometimes she didn't remember him. His love for Sue was so great that it amazed me, but I also could see the hurt of not being able to communicate with her that was taking a toll on his emotions.

Sue's husband substituted manly conversation in place of the intimate conversation that he was missing with Sue. He would meet with the boys every afternoon in town for a meal. Sue lived in her own world that consisted mainly of strangers, venturing out for only minutes at a time. One minute she was meeting you for the first time that resulted in a very formal introduction of kindness. In a split second, that minute would pass and you were once again a stranger in her home. I spent more time running away from Sue than anything else. Thank goodness that the living room, dining room, front entrance, and kitchen had no doors that closed off any one section to any of the rooms as it formed a circle around the fireplace in the living room. I referred to this as my own little mouse wheel inside their home, my cage while on duty.

It wasn't unusual to find pictures wrapped in clothes and placed under the bathroom sink.

At times, Sue was like a scavenger, everything she touched could be found in one of the bathroom cabinets. One day I saw Sue trying to take a picture off the wall in the living room and suggested that it looked nice on the wall. This statement only made Sue angrier as she continued to channel her new frustration, me, into getting the picture down without any success. After Sue left the picture, I went over to see why Sue couldn't remove it from the wall and found that her husband had screwed the picture to the wall.

It was very hard to plan daily activities like cook meals, get her bathed, or even dressed. On this one particular day, Sue's husband wanted her to get some fresh air and sunshine and asked if I would take her out on the front porch to sit for a little while. I didn't see anything wrong with that so I said yes. Sue's home was the last house at the end of the block with a four-way stop. As we sat on the front porch watching the cars pass I noticed that one particular driver seemed lost or not paying attention as he approached the four-way stop. He caught Sue's attention with the sound of screeching tires when he stopped suddenly. Sue jumped from her chair on the front porch like a marathon runner as she rushed down the steps, off the porch running for the road. Sue's hands were made into fists as she screamed, "get out, get out, get out" at the driver. I was afraid that Sue would go into the road and she did just that. I rushed across the front lawn into the road and stood between her and the car. Traffic had stopped but not Sue. She was still in the road when I took hold of her arm trying to stop…. POW…. stars, I never saw her fist coming. I realized then that Sue was chasing the car and I couldn't stop her. My words fell on deaf ears. I suddenly yelled b***h as loud as I could. As I had hoped, this stopped her dead in her tracks. She turned back towards me. I was now her target. I continuously yelled the B word over and over which caused her to keep her eyes locked on me and not the road. I was running, screaming the B word, and praising God all at the same time as I made my way out of the road and into the driveway. I would ask forgiveness later but for this moment, I had to get her out of the street and back to the front porch. Sue was out of the road. We were going for the home stretch as we approached the front porch. I found myself wondering, how will I get her into the house. Her foot rested on the very last step going onto the porch; if I can only get her into the house. Come on Sue, come get me, come on you B… She had one hand on the rail, one foot on the porch, and one foot up in the air, only a short distance to go, just step up onto the porch. I had the front door open not knowing what or how I would get her into the house, when honk, honk. If I could cuss without a conscience, I would have out cussed a sailor that day even thought I don't know how much a sailor cuss'. A car had stopped in the road and was honking the horn at a dog, yes a dog right in front of the house. Remember those issues I mentioned in chapter one, well this particular dog was now an issue too. Sue ran down those four steps with all the vigor of a twenty year old after the dog or the car. I have never talked to anyone so fast using such vulgar language only to be totally ignored. Crying for fear that Sue would be run over like a dog/reindeer.

James 3: 1-2

1 Not many of you should become teachers, my brothers, for you realize that we will be judged more strictly, 2 for we all fall short in many respects. If no one falls short in speech, he is a perfect man, able to bridle his whole body also.

I continued to run circles around Sue calling her names, grabbing at her clothes only to be swatted at like a nat; nothing and I mean nothing pierced her mental thoughts from trying to catch that dog/car. God was watching over us and sent an angel just as I had lost hope. The mother of Sue's daughter-in-law drove past us in the road and realized what was taking place, she quickly returned. This lady's car pulled into the driveway and blew the horn, thank you Lord for small miracles. Sue turned her attention to the person honking her horn at her in her driveway. Sue did not recognize who this stranger was. Then this stranger asked to use the phone. Sue offered this stranger a cup of tea; I couldn't believe that Sue was inviting her in. This stranger introduced herself as a friend of the family and thought that I might need some company until Sue's husband came home. It was Sue's last trip to the front yard. The rest of her outings were moved to the fenced in backyard where Sue enjoyed sitting under the cherry tree that spring without being disturbed.

Sue normally loved to shower but on this particular day, I don't know what caused her retreat from the shower, maybe it was the water temperature or even the water pressure. You never really knew what would cause Sue to revolt at any time or place. Sue is in the shower, I was washing her hair when she started to panic and wanted out of the shower. I knew that if she got out of the shower I would never get the soap off her body and out of her hair. I checked the water again to make sure it was not to hot or cold and closed the shower door back. The shower door was clear plastic as Sue and I watched each other, maybe that was it. Did she see me as a stranger who was going to attack her while she showered? I knew she was safe so I sang to drown out her screams of protest. I'm not a great singer but I always sang to calm my children when they were babies so I gave it my best shot. I sang my best bathtub voice ever. As I sang, she stopped screaming. I continued to sing and then Sue began to sing along with me. You guessed it; I started singing each time before Sue got into the shower and continued until she was finished.

Sue was getting dressed as usual on this fine summer day. We were in the bedroom as she had just finished picking out what she wanted to wear when a robin perched on the windowsill that caught Sue's attention. The first bird we had seen this spring. The robin flew as Sue crossed the room. I managed to get Sue to return to the chair to put on her stockings (pantyhose) which was the first time that she had requested to wear them since I had been with her. I'm squatting at her feet with the stockings pulled up to her knees when Sue asked me, "Do you like wearing these?"

Have you ever had the feeling that no matter how you answer a question, that the answer will be wrong? I knew this was one of those times as I answered her question with no. Sue replied, "Then why should I?" I was lucky this time. I saw the right hand make into a fist and blocked the blow by catching her wrist inches away from my face. Even though I blocked her fist, Sue managed to send me to the floor onto my bottom. To be in her late eighties, she had the strength of a young man.

I jumped to my feet and managed to get Sue to sit down in the chair. She had the stockings pulled up to her knees and she did not have enough balance to walk with them that way or the mental ability to finish pulling them up or down. With safety being a major concern, I knew the stockings had to come off. The problem, she would not let me come near her; I was the stranger in the house again. I couldn't leave the room, so we waited this dilemma out. Thirty minutes later another robin landed on the windowsill of the bedroom. I seized the moment and turned the stranger back into a friend that provided the opportunity to change the fate of this pair of pantyhose.

Rest those merry silks of olden gold
Buried deep beneath the folds
In the bottom of the closet
Never to rise to stardom again
Those cursed things
Called pantyhose

Sue's husband had left as usual this particular morning but she followed him to the front door as he said goodbye. Time had come for the need to lock all windows and doors to prevent Sue from wondering off again; Sue was now an escape artist. Normally I would lock the door and put the key on the ledge above it, but this particular day Sue was watching, so I placed the key in my pocket after locking the door. Sue walked to the front door and tried to open it. Becoming frustrated, she turned to me and said, "Give me the key." Shocked, I responded, "I don't have the key" and turned to walk away when Sue grabbed my arm turning me completely around facing her. She looked straight into my eyes and said very harshly, "You liar. It is in your pocket." After her words vanished into the air only silence penetrated the hall between us, each waiting for the other to say a word or make a move. Then Sue stepped forward and stomped her foot on the floor to make a point. The look in her eyes let me know that I had to get away from her fast. I started backing up slowly until I thought that it was safe enough to turn and run, but I was not fast enough. Sue had me. I felt her hands in my hair as she began to tighten her grip. I knew that I was in danger due to previously being bitten and scratched, which required a tetanus shot. I knew that I had to protect myself and Sue, which required no broke skin, hers, nor mine. Thank you Lord for quick thinking, I screamed fire, fire pointing towards the kitchen. Sue for one moment froze, and then I made my get away as she released her grip on my hair and began looking for the fire.

The little mouse wheel that I described earlier that consisted of the living room, dining room, kitchen, and front hall that were open to each other as they circled an enormous fireplace became the path that maintained my sanity. Sue had progressed to a state where everyone was always the stranger and she never stopped chasing them. One particular day, Sue seemed to be unmanageable as she refused to give up the chaise around my mouse wheel. Most of the time you were able to maintain a safe distance ahead or behind her, just staying in her sight to make sure that she remained safe. Usually after five to ten minutes into the chase, Sue would usually give up. Not this day though, Sue and I danced around each other like boxers sparing around the ring as I kept her in eyesight but out of reach insuring that she didn't put me down for the count. Sue would not give up the chase nor could I change her mental thinking. For over an hour, we went round and round the circle. I remained the stranger in her house and she was determined to catch me. I was so tired from the chase but Sue did not seem to be tiring at all. I had to do something, the bathroom. Why didn't I think of that before? I made sure that Sue saw me enter the bathroom and then I pulled down my pants and sat on the commode. No slip-ups, Sue still paid attention to details and sure enough she shoved opened the bathroom door. She looked directly at me, staring me up and down as I sat with bare butt upon the throne. When she realized I was actually in the process of using the bathroom I said with enthusiasm, "Excuse me, do you mind if I finish using the bathroom?" Sue's face flushed with embarrassment and said, "I'm so sorry, please let me know when you are finished, I have to go to the bathroom too." I could hear Sue fidgeting outside the bathroom m door so I rested for a few minutes and then pulled myself together and walked out the bathroom where she was waiting.

I said a silent prayer; please Lord give me the strength to run. Instead, Sue looked at me, replied, "It's my turn" and walked into the bathroom. I took advantage of the moment and gave her a bath.

Never has a client touched my heart as deeply as Sue did. In the front hall of Sue's home hung a huge wall mirror at least four foot wide by six foot long. Over the previous year, we walked by this mirror many, many times, but this time as we passed, Sue paused in front of the mirror. She seemed puzzled at first and began to investigate the reflection of herself in the mirror closer. Looking back at Sue was an old woman. Sue studied every inch of that person in the mirror for quite some time and then with her finger she traced the persons' face. I couldn't figure out what Sue was doing so I remained quietly behind her. Then I watched Sue try to touch each wrinkle on the face of the older woman in the mirror. Then she pointed at the older woman and asked, "Is that me?" The question held as much confusion to Sue as her voice implied. I answered her question with a simple yes. I then witnessed Sue's realization that the older woman was actually her. A sad look came over Sue's face as tears formed in her eyes and rolled over her checks to the floor. My tears joined hers, but for a different reason on that day. I realized that I could also be Sue one day. I saw myself that day in another time, in a different place, in a world all of my own too in that mirror. Just as quick, as the tears had rolled off of Sue's cheek and disappeared into the carpet also did the moment that Sue realized whom she had become. A place called the golden years.

Sue remained in her home with her husband until a room in the nursing home became available. Her husband had become a total stranger to her and the object of abuse. Everyone in Sue's world had become strangers.

Has Alzheimer's ever had an impact on your life?

How?

_____

_____

_____

_____

_____

_____

_____

_____

What kind of emotional battles do you think families of Alzheimer's go through as they try to keep their loved one in their home?

_____

_____

_____

_____

_____

_____

_____

_____

_____

What kind of assistance could you help provide to family members of an Alzheimer patient; more direct how can you help them with a stranger that lives within someone else's body?

_____

_____

_____

Luke 9: 1-2
1 He summoned the Twelve and gave them power and authority over all daemons and to cure diseases, 2 and he sent them to proclaim the kingdom of God and to heal [the sick].

Exodus 15:26 If you really listen to the voice of the LORD, your God," he told them, "and do what is right in his eyes: if you heed his commandments and keep all his precepts, I will not afflict you with any of the diseases with which I afflicted the Egyptians; for I the Lord, am your healer.

I pray that I can remain faithful to the Lord.

Maybe you saw yourself in Sue as I did. The clients I have worked with have many types of diseases and ailments. My spiritual journey grew because I allowed people to touch my life and I applied God's word that gave valuable wisdom when needed. I chose not to judge the person for as the Bible also tells us, do not judge unless you also are judged.

A SECRET SISTER

By: Donna Robbins

Unlike our blood sister
She's a friend formed from an innate relationship
A special confidant

She brings mystical moments into your life
At times, she seems more than an acquaintance
She possesses passion that reveals to you she is hidden
Stirring interest in the nameless companion

She goes the extra mile to inspire you in some way

As to arouse that baffling desire called, sisterhood
To see if you are thinking about her today

As we turn to the moment of mystical adventure
You will find that you could be that secret sister

Apart from receiving, what do you give back
In each other's mind
Remembered elegantly, we wish

Unique as if we were one of a kind
No one else can understand
By human reasoning alone

But rather as an executor of the sister
That lives within each of us
Sharing that special bond
Called sisterly love

Sirach 25:1-3 Those Who Are Worthy of Praise
1 With three things I am delighted, for they are pleasing to the Lord and to men: Harmony among brethren, friendship among neighbors,

Donna Robbins

and the mutual love of husband and wife. 2 Three kinds of men I hate; their manner of life I loathe indeed: A proud pauper, a rich dissembler, and an old man lecherous in his dotage. 3 What you have not saved in your youth, how will you acquire in your old age?

Adam & Eve

By: Donna Robbins

Love
A place in the heart of one who cares
It lets another person know that they are safe
An act of sharing experiences
It keeps each from domination
As they walk hand in hand together

A leader can't follow
A follower can't lead

In bedlam
Only confusion is the discoverer

A delicate flower of any species cannot bloom
Without the aspect of love
As it yearns for sensitivity
Longing to belong only to one

Love flees at the sound of glacial ice moving
through unknown waters
As it explores forbidden places to the end of
time

To dwell harmoniously
In the one temple
That two have begun to interweave

To complete the transformation
That God planned for a creature named Man
Therefore, woman came to exist
Joined as one

CHAPTER 6

The Enjoyable, The wicked, and The Aggressive

Matthew 7: 13, 14

13 "Enter through the narrow gate; for the gate is wide and the road broad that leads to destruction, and those who enter through it are many. 14 How narrow the gate and constricted the road that leads to life. And those who find it are few.

After moving to Niagara Falls, New York, I learned that New York State would not honor or accept my South Carolina's Nursing Assistant Certification (CNA). I had to retake the Nursing Assistant course. The difference between the blue book of the south and the blue book of the north was as different as day and night. In 1990, I was accepted into a CNA position at one of the Nursing facilities in NF, N.Y. and was hired full time after I passed my clinical.

Over a ten week period this course provided us newbie's (new recruits) over the 90 hours of classroom instruction and 40 hours of work experience required at that facility compared to the south that required only thirty-five hours and no clinical.

This was my first time working in a nursing home, which is often referred to as the Old Folk's Home. Over the years, I have heard horror stories about nursing homes that I never believed until I actually worked in one. The things that I am going to tell you are real concerning my first experiences working in a nursing home. I hope you will believe them but if you chose not to I understand, because as I said, I was in denial too about the stories that I had heard until I lived them.

After a week of classroom lectures, we began covering classroom material in the mornings and in the afternoons we worked under the supervision of a full time aide. In the nursing home the term floor, which I will keep referring to, simply means that the nursing home is divided into sections and the aides are assigned to residents in a particular section of the floor.

We spent hours making beds; I even caught myself making my bed at home like those I made in the nursing home. Then we moved on to helping the full time aides feed the clients/patients/residents that were not capable of feeding themselves; my first time feeding another human being besides my children. I am not by nature a quiet person and I have a dominating personality. I grew up inferior under the control of men in my life simply because they believed women had no rights. I am a rebel at heart and because of man's control, my soul fought to find contentment as I grew into the woman that I wanted to become. I thought that I had left those shackles of control behind only to find them again in the eyes of women and men within the walls of confinement in this place, the nursing home. I watched the resident's faces and reactions. I saw how hard they were fighting to overcome the fear that the full time aides had instilled into them. Some still voiced their feelings, as they shouted "NO" when approached. Others were crying as the full time aide's shoved food into their mouths. The tears that I saw were from their hearts that expressed, I am no longer free. Not until later did I understand that I was just beginning to grow into the woman that God wanted me to be.

Freedom

By: Donna Robbins

Birds are free
Are we

They live from day to day
No minds they have so we say
But God gave them a special design
Let's look closer so we can see

From spring time of abundance
To winter of barren lands
They don't wait till another finds the worm

Donna Robbins

To be fed

They take only what they need
Leaving a trail for others to find
From new songs to empty nests each spring

That chirp is to God
That you hear them sing
A thank you for all they have
Not chirps of what they have missed

No minds they have
So you say
Or do they

Birds are free
Are we

1 Peter 2:15-17
15 For it is the will of God that by doing good
you may silence the ignorance of foolish people.
16 Be free, yet without using freedom as a
pretext for evil, but as slaves of God. 17 Give

honor to all, love the community, fear God, honor the king.

Classmates realized how disgusted I was with the total lack of patience that the full time aides demonstrated with the residents, especially when they were trying to feed them their meals. The full time aides picked up on my disgust too, so one day they asked the nurse on duty to assign me to a resident that I had never seen before. The aides fed this particular resident in her room. My comrades thought I needed to be taught a lesson and took great joy knowing that I was assigned to her and they made it known as they passed along the information that this resident was blind, did not talk, and took great pleasure in hitting and biting the aide. Is the picture coming together for you?

I asked the aides what this resident's name was as I took her tray out of their hands and walked into her room. I quickly placed one of her hands over the other with mine on top, just in case. I began talking to her and quickly realized that talking only made her angry. I realized that she had been talked at, too much. I didn't know how to gain her trust since words only made her angrier each time I spoke. So I did the only other thing that I knew to do, sing. Singing had always been my way of coping with my children during sickness, tiredness, and with other clients in the past. Singing was a tool that I used to control my own emotions. I instantly realized as I sang that it was the calmness she needed and watched a window open that gave her new sight in her blindness. As I sang she began to listen, then she started swaying with the words; where my singing took her, I will never know.

As I sung, "Rock of ages cleft for me, let me hide myself in thee" this southern girl touched that northern blind soul. The raging fire of raw emotions in that room changed to a valley of contentment with peace for both of us. I then sung from my soul and fed this beautiful resident her meal. After she finished her meal, she rewarded me with a simple smile that spoke a thousand words. The window of trust opened unto me and I took complete advantage of it. I was proud as I walked back into the hall with an empty tray. The other aides were confused, but then confusion turned to fury. The aides realized that I had accomplished what they could not. The aides then told the nurse that I had eaten her food, see this lady's tray came back every day almost untouched. No one believed that she ate all of her food. At the next meal, I was watched by the nurse to see how I had managed to get her to eat. The aides last comments were, "Well, don't expect me to sing to her."

In the health care field, death and dying are a part of the business too. In fact, the five stages of death: denial, anger, bargaining, depression, and acceptance are also tools that we use. These tools help the HHA/CNA to understand to some degree what our clients are going through. Have you ever touched a dead body or held a human body as life drained from it? When a loved one dies suddenly, you may find yourself going through these stages too. I will provide a short overview of each one from my perspective.

Denial is straight forward. You deny that this can happen to you. Sometimes it is simply a state of shock that progresses into a lack of meaninglessness and you become overwhelmed. Family members use denial to provide them with strength to get through their loved ones' death sometimes; for me, it was a year after my dad's death that it became a reality for me and that I accepted that he was truly absent from my life. As I look back I now see that God granted me the grace of denial until I could handle my own emotions of dad's death, because otherwise I don't know if I could have remained strong for my mother as she grieved.

Anger offers a fight and/or flight stage that justifies your emotions. Anger offers healing if used correctly until you can accept your own death or that of your loved one. I have often seen the client suppress their anger until it seems that it is consuming them because they blame God.

Also, healthcare professionals are not immune from the death of their clients. In our career, we pretend that we don't get attached to our clients, but we do.

Bargaining is usually what the client does after they get over the shock that they are going to die or the death of a loved one. Many of my clients while on their deathbeds usually admitted to me openly after they realized that I was Christian that they want to make a deal with God. Also I have heard family members trying to make a deal with God, if He would only bring them back. During this stage, I was asked the most questions about my faith and God, even if they had walked with God for many years. If I were given the diagnosis that I was going to die soon, I wouldn't want the doctor to give me a death sentence that equals to number of days, months, or years. What about you?

In this stage, I tried to accept my fathers' death and I asked God many questions. What if I had gone back to SC would it have made a difference? What if I had called him more often would it have made a difference? What if I had, if I had, if I had…… As much as I wanted to go back in time, I realized that I needed to cling to my memories instead of letting them slip away with questions that had no answers.

Depression was a breeze for me because it let my feelings of hurt have meaning. For my clients though I watched them struggle as they tried to accept death. Most of my clients were depressed because they knew they were leaving someone they cared about very deeply behind. This is the most painful stage to watch your client go through. There are more tears than there are tissues in this stage.

Acceptance is the stage that offers the ability to smile again. You begin to experience things on a renewed level. You can listen to what your spouse, children, siblings, friends, and community have to say or not say. The dying comforts the living. When I accepted my father's death I experienced a rush of feelings that I had suppressed for a year; I knew then that I was going to be alright without him. Just because there are five stages, that doesn't always mean that a person will go through all of them and sometimes I feel that there are more than these five.

Have you ever experienced the death of a loved one? If so, write down what you remember.

_____

_____

_____

_____

_____

_____

_____

If you have a weak stomach, you might want to skip this section as I describe preparing the body after death. The first dead body that I examined and helped the aide prepare before the coroner arrived and pronounce them dead provided a different view of death than I was prepared for. During death, the body releases fluids. The eyes and mouth are closed and a rolled washcloth or towel placed under the chin to keep the mouth closed until rigor mortis occurs. The arms are folded over the chest or stomach and a sheet tucked under the body to hold them in place.

This body was already cold and stiff when our class arrived into resident's the room. The skin color fades with death. My other classmates thought that I was mad as I began lifting the sheet to examine the body fully from head to toe. They could not conceive the fact that it did not bother me being in the room or touching the corpse. There were different emotions that each of us experienced in that half-hour of preparing the corpse after the sting of death.

The only thing that weighed deeply on my feelings concerning this experience was the fact that I had to leave the draped sheet covering this person's face. It became final with this act: the conclusion of a life that was no longer on this earth. Is she in heaven? Is she sitting at the throne of God? Is she connecting with loved ones? What do you think?

_____

_____

_____

_____

_____

_____

This story's perceptive is from an upside down point of view. This particular lady in the nursing home liked to wear men's briefs. Nothing unusual in today's society but sixteen or more years ago it might have seemed strange to find a woman in man's underwear. On that particular day many years ago, I did not say a word out loud but my face must have said something without me realizing. I had heard of men wearing women's underwear and people who wore no underwear but a woman in man's briefs, I remember thinking, just different, no more or no less. Well she must have thought that I was judging her like so many other aides had previously done. I also believe that at that moment she determined to make me pay for judging her.

We went into the shower room and I proceeded to give her a shower. With her, we had to use a special shower chair with wheels that took the place of the wheelchair. I don't remember the reason why she was only to have showers, but I finished lathering her upper body with a special soap that we used only for her and rinsed her body with precisely the right water temperature. I washed her legs and then bent down to wash her feet when I felt her hand in my hair. Just as quick, her other hand slipped into my hair with a grip that brought forth a scream from me.

The joke was on me though; I was the one standing on my head, upside down. As I kept trying to get free from her grip, she kept my head bobbing up and down like a cork in water. With each jerk, my head came closer to the floor. I remember thinking, what if she pushed me to the floor onto my knees. If she did, I would lose all my leverage both physically and mentally.

The million dollar question, how do I get out of this predicament? I tried pleading with her, which resulted in her grip tightening with each word I spoke. My screams flooded the empty halls that at other times were full of people, aides, and excitement. I truly felt helpless and trapped. Is this how a baby animal feels when we have them in our hands trying to play with them? Just holding them (baby animal) ever so tight where they can't run away from us; their hearts pounding wildly as fear takes over. No, oh no that's when the heart has a panic attack.

Matthew 7: 1-5

1 "Stop judging, that you may not be judged. 2 For as you judge, so will you be judged, and the measure with which you measure will be measured out to you." 3 Why do you notice the splinter in your brother's eye, but do not perceive the wooden beam in your own eye? 4 How can you say to your brother, "Let me remove that splinter from your eye, while the wooden beam is in your eye? 5 You hypocrite, remove the wooden beam from your eye first;

then you will see clearly to remove the splinter from your brothers eye.

I must do something. I grabbed her wrist trying to apply enough pressure to make her let go of my hair. I forgot about the soap that was still on my hands as I attempted to squeeze her wrists even tighter. Nothing was happening but a lot of slipping and sliding to her own laughter. My eyes started to burn from the soap that was dripping down my arms into my face. Out of sheer frustration, I screamed harder and harder praying that an aide would hear me. My screams became hoarse sounds that echoed through the empty halls causing an avalanche of fear within this room.

Mentally I ran through my options, how much longer could I stand on my head? How much longer till an aide comes down this hall for whatever reason? I told myself to stop playing the IF game. I realized I had no concrete answers so I visualized getting wet but I would be free. I chose wet and free as I took the sprayer and rinsed my hands free of the soap. Was the sprayer long enough to reach her from this upside down position. Without hesitation, I grabbed the shower chair, pulled it close just in case the sprayer was too short, and turned the sprayer on the lady. She just laughed.

Okay Donna, make sure the water is warm and spray her again. I counted to three, took a deep breath, and aimed. I felt her grip. She was pulling my hair out of my scalp. I took hold of her wrist again and squeezed with every ounce of strength I had. It was all in vain. She was stronger than I had anticipated as she held me in this precarious position. She continued to tighten her grip. The pain made me cry. Alarm bells were ringing loudly in my brain, when a storm suddenly arrived, a brainstorm of an idea that is; why didn't I think of that in the first place. I turned the water to full blast, but this time the water was ice cold and I aimed straight for this lovely lady's face.

Repercussions of total shock escaped from her lips. She managed to remove more hair from my scalp as she pulled away but I was free, free at last. The echo of our screams joined as they flooded the halls breaking the Dead Sea of Silence. As I stood up straight, someone finally walked through the door. I was amused by the look on the other aide's face as I stood there soaking wet. I pushed this lovely lady's shower chair back against the far wall and proceeded to wash my own hair and then I went on with my day's work. After this incident, I began checking where my client's hands were before bending over to wash any body part. Funny how things look totally different when you are upside down, anyone for pineapple upside down cake.

This next resident was a poseur who loved to sit just outside the elevator doors. She was a small, dainty woman with a husky voice that sounded more like a man than a woman. She greeted everyone who stepped off of the elevator but if you were a male she did everything in her power to make them stay and talk, even tug at the sleeve to get their attention as she greeted them with a slow, drawn out c...o...m...e... - o...n... (come on). She reminded me of a cat purring and yearning to be stroked. She made gentleman blush and their lady friends mad. We named her Houdini because of her magical reappearance to the elevator. You could put her in her room or you could put her in another hallway far away from the elevator and without anyone seeing her, she would be back in a chair at the elevator within minutes. There was one other piece to this lady that was just as mysterious. I have never seen anyone who could undress their self as fast as she could. She either hated clothes or had other ideas. I'm not sure if either of these choices was correct but I am sure of this, you could not keep her dressed, she always stripped down to her undergarments even though we never gave up trying.

I am finding that the older I get, I join her choice not to wear clothes. I wonder if I am turning into a Houdini too since I find great joy in my birthday suit as I age. Hope I choose a warmer climate to retire, depending upon this fact.

Romans 14:13 Then let us no longer judge one another, but rather resolve never to put a stumbling block or hindrance in the way of a brother.

After a tiring day of work, I arrived home. I had slipped into something more comfortable for the evening when my daughter announced that we needed milk. My daughter went with me to the store. We parked beside this car that had a sign in the window that read, "SMILE IF YOUR'E NOT WEARING UNDERWEAR!" I almost wet my panties. What panties? Just remember, don't judge the person by the underwear that they are in.

Threads of cotton, nylon, or lace all woven into the perfect place
Housed beneath this web of woe
Sporting someone's thoughts of another
Of how we should be dressed to travel to and fro
With this garment of man's design
COMES
Anguish too many that find

They don't have to follow the eras of man's ways
Their so called golden rules that they try to apply
In the form of underwear

My daughter smiled graciously at me after she read the sign in the car window and then asked, "Mom, are you wearing underwear." Both of us then enjoyed the best laugh ever; we both did not have on any underwear. No we are not mad, insane, women of the street or cracked pots. We just smile more at the end of the day than most. SMILE if you are not wearing underwear!

The following events lead me to believe the nursing assistant's greatest danger is from other aides, not the residents in the nursing home. A small percentage of the residents can be dangerous but most are great. One comment frequently directed towards us from the permanent aides at the nursing facility when we worked with them on the floor was, "Once they get on the floor full time we'll break them in right." I didn't take this comment serious until a short time later. Another senior aide threatened me on the job because I refused to do the job the way that she showed me. It was nothing like what I had learned in class. Short cuts did not even come close to describing how she expected me to do this particular part of the job.

I was informed I would be met outside and she would show me who the boss was. All because I refused to conform to the way that the full time aides performed their jobs and continued to perform my tasks the way that we were taught in class. Us newbie's made the senior aides look bad, because we performed the job in the same amount of time that they did, but with greater proficiency. I stood my ground, tattled to the supervisor on duty, and watched my back from that day forward. Over the next few months us newbie's performed our jobs at a faster pace than the full time aides and without short cuts. Those hours of class time seemed like months before completion.

Us newbie's were assigned to permanent floors of the nursing home once we passed our clinical exams. Then the North Wind blew into the nursing home in the form of a licensed practical nurse (LPN) right out of school onto the floor that I was assigned. She had the backbone of a jellyfish. The senior aides subjugated her within two weeks of being on the job to their way of thinking. This new LPN was the tool that the full time aides would use to overpower us newbie's who had just finished training as they began to enforce their preference of how we would do our job.

This LPN did a great job on all of us. She made us newbie's shake in our boots. Then the day came that her rule broke my spirit and love for my job. This LPN made me so mad that I could not rationalize the circumstance that she had just put me in. I will try to explain. I was working with this patient who had a bowel movement while in her bed and it was everywhere; on the bed, on her, and under her nails. I had managed to get the bed and patient cleaned of all feces except for under her nails, which were packed full of bowel movement. I had gone to the nurses' station and got a few nail sticks that we used to clean under the patients finger nails. I had just finished one of the patient's hands and had begun to work on the other, when the door to this patient's room burst wide open. I was thankful that the other resident in the room had left only a few minutes before the North Wind/ LPN had entered. The LPN was inches away from my face shouting, "How dare you take the time to clean nails. You have other people that need to washed and dressed before breakfast. There is no time for this." On and on she went and then I began to cry.

A hot southern wind (me) blew the Northern Wind (LPN) back to the North Pole. I didn't tell her exactly what I thought of her then and there, but the north wind knew that the sky had darkened and that she had unleashed a tempest within the nursing home that day. You have heard the saying, "The straw that broke the camel's back," well my resignation letter would have broken any heart as it brought forth all the cruel things that the aides and nurses did to each other and to the people they took care of. I knew that I had to leave this brutality that went on between co-workers. I ended my employment with them while I still felt that I had a heart, especially if I wanted to continue helping others.

Song of Songs 4: 16 Arise, north wind! Come, south wind! Blow upon my garden that its perfumes may spread abroad.

In Greek mythology, Boreas was the name of the god that represented the north wind and Notos was the name of the god that represented the south wind.

1st Timothy 4:8 for, while physical training is of limited value, devotion is valuable in every respect, since it holds a promise of life both for the present life and for the future.

Later on, I realized that I had left the nursing home hastily. I would have to return to this place, the nursing home due to finances, but I chose a different nursing home than the one that I had left.

CHAPTER 7

Dirty or Clean

In this chapter, I will discuss my experiences working with human beings that had issues with housekeeping skills that displayed the extreme side of dirty and clean. Over the past 15 plus or minus years, ninety-five percent of client's homes that I visited fell between two spectrums, dirty or clean; by clean I mean live able with some clutter and dirty means unwashed dishes and clothes, floors that need sweeping/mopping, everything in chaos. Unfortunately, the other five percent are on the extreme side of dirty or clean, as you will come to understand.

Dirty! What do you really think of when you hear this word?

_____

_____

_____

_____

When I stated dirty, did you think that I meant a person that hadn't washed their clothes, or that they smelled of body odor, or maybe even a trash can that smelled? Maybe you thought of a house where things are out of place or the kitchen was messy. This is what I meant by dirty. This particular case the client's second floor apartment was beyond the imagination of the word dirty. Her entire bedroom floor was piled with clothes at least one and half to two feet deep, except for an alleyway around her bed. When I picked up a washcloth and towel that she instructed me to use for her bath, fleas jumped all over us; each room in her home was the same or worse. In the living-room, the path for her wheelchair stopped in front of the television. Another smaller path connected to this larger path that was about a foot and half wide that continued the entire length of the couch that her friend used. No other areas of the floor in the living room were visible due to clothes, trash, etc. piled as high as three to four feet high. She had her dog locked in the bathroom. In the kitchen is where she requested to have her bath because of the dog's location. I could not see the dog but his bark informed me that I didn't want to meet him. At the kitchen sink though, her friendly guest greeted me; the cockroach family were enjoying their breakfast. They looked up from their morning meal to say hello and continued to eat. I had to disturb their breakfast so that I could bath my client and prepare her breakfast, but they didn't go very far.

The morning sun burst through the kitchen windows from the enclosed porch caught my attention. That would be a delightful place to sit with her (my client) while she ate her breakfast. I decided that I would surprise her and serve her breakfast on the porch. I opened the door to the porch; remember we are on the second floor. I almost stepped into a hole. As I surveyed the enclosed porch, I saw holes everywhere in the top layer of wood floorboards from piles of dog dung and urine stains that were clearly visible. As I took in the stench, I gagged. The thought of breakfast on the enclosed porch became transient as I decided that the kitchen with the cockroaches was a better place to serve breakfast. I befuddled my client when I refused to join her for breakfast. I could see in her eyes that she was hurt because I did not join her for a cup of coffee. I truthfully explained that it was company policy that we not partake of food or drink with the client. She then informed me that the other aide always joined her for coffee. I knew she was watching me and I also knew that my actions resembled someone that was standing in a bed of hot coals. I told her I had to prepare the kitchen for her bath. I rushed through my job that day and finished in record time.

Would you have had coffee with her? Do you think that you could be her permanent aide three times a week? What do you think? Be honest!

_____

_____

_____

_____

_____

_____

_____

Matthew 7: 12 "Do to others whatever you would have them do to you. This is the law and the prophets.

I left there that day with a guilty conscience. All the way to the car, I justified my actions. I was scared to get in my car. I didn't know what uninvited guest of hers could be hitching a ride home with me. In fact, I did have a guest that came home with me that day; he was a demon that carried seeds of judgment so cleverly disguised as filth. I rushed straight home that day unaware of the stranger that filled my heart with ammunition that made me feel comfortable with my actions. After arriving home, I showered and scrubbed myself from head to toe. After I showered I was faced with a major decision, do I burn my clothes or bleach them. Instead, I choose to throw them out. I then went to my employer and informed them that I would not be taking this case on a permanent basis as I had originally agreed to. My supervisor informed me that I had already accepted the case and that I would not be taken off of it. I then asked my supervisor if the nurse that opened this case knew that it was filthy to the degree that I described to her and the reply was yes. I told my employer that they did not inform me of the condition of this client's home when this case was offered. Therefore, they had a choice, take me off the case or accept my resignation. I was taken off the case. Years later, I realized that those seeds of judgment that the demon had planted in my heart that day had matured and they had to be pulled from their filthy hiding place.

DID YOU

By: Donna Robbins-April of 1994

As I ended this day like so many before
I said my prayers
But heard this knock at my door

Opened my eyes
A voice says look

Donna Robbins

Your breakfast was a shambles
Your lunch made you sick
Your dinner sits there just like a brick

Over in the corner sits three loads of clothes
To be washed and dried
Three more loads to fold

Dust on your coffee table
Provides a place to draw a face
Not one thing straight or in its place
Not a broom or mop has touched these floors
Plates and cups cover the counter top
The trashcan flows over the brim
Glass doors smeared with children's' kisses
Your lawn uncut and filled with weeds

Then a loud voice said
Take another look
Breakfast, you didn't start off with God
The way you could have
Lunch, you didn't even ask God to bless a crumb
Dinner, you didn't care to feast
On what God would provide

Over in the corner sat three souls
That you didn't take the time to witness to
If you had,
They may have been washed clean
With God's love

Three other souls sat there that you rushed by
You could have made a difference
In which path they would have took

Every thought and care
Running around wild and loose
Bringing problems to the soul
In some way or another
Because they were not put in their place
Like the face in the dust
Our souls put on a sad face
When not wiped clean at the end of the day

Oh, the dirt that gets under foot
With neglect

I am scared to look at what I might see
I am in need of cleaning out my own soul

Of all the sins I didn't address
As they now try to take over me
As I failed to take care of them

So blinded by all my own mistakes
Oh Lord
I think it is time that I clean house

Clean! What do you think of when you hear this word?

_____

_____

_____

_____

_____

Did you think that I meant everything was put away nice and neat? This is what I mean by cleanness equals insanity. A person hands you a mask and booties like those you see in the doctor's office when greeted at the front door. This person who greeted you then informs you very politely that they don't want you to breathe your germs on them. You find yourself standing there alone with a mask in one hand, a pair of booties in the other hand, when you hear these words, "Also please leave your shoes and belongings outside. There is a box where you can place your things" as she points to a big chest. "The combination to the lock is ## - ### - ##."

As you stand there with the supplies in your hands, you wonder why you couldn't just put the booties on over your shoes and not put your shoes in the box. What are you thinking? in the box. What are you thinking?

_____

_____

_____

_____

_____

Well my thoughts ran wild as I thought about what kind of conditions I might be heading into. As I walked through the door, this lady was standing there very patiently in the hall and greeted me with a disposable gown and a hair net. Her words stunned me, "We don't want any of your lose hair to fall on the floor."

My client had already been bathed, dressed, and was seated in the living area before I arrived. I was handed a pan and bottle of bleach solution to wash down the bed, walls, and floor of this client's room. There was a plastic cover over the mattress that I was instructed to wipe with the bleach solution. After preparing the meal, everything in the kitchen including all appliances that I touched had to be washed with the bleach solution. I wondered as I left there could I have taken something with me and I rush straight home once again to wash myself with a bleach solution.

This time I am going to ask you to write down what seeds that demon could have left behind in my heart that would grow into plants or weeds that I would have to take care of later.

_____

_____

_____

_____

CHAPTER 8

What's on The Menu?

This chapter deals with a very touchy subject, weight. I will explore this subject from a self-portrait view, not what a set of scales reflect. In the twentieth-century, there are a lot of people and companies that view human beings by a set of scales created for appropriate weight. Along with these scales, man produced a weight chart that reflects what society still considers the average weight for all human beings. By this, I mean that the majority of humans, businesses, doctors, and government have an opinion concerning the weight of other people in regards to what they should weigh without concern for the human beings mental wellbeing.

Man has destroyed man since the beginning of time mostly because of selfish motives that one human has placed upon another human. Man has created a set of standards for all of mankind called the norm in regards to what the outside of the human being is to look like, but nowhere did they use any of God's measuring tools to form this assessment. Those norms have bounced from one end of the spectrum to the other throughout history.

Proverbs 11:1 False scales are an abomination to the LORD, but a full weight is his delight.

Standards for weight have always been interesting. A simple component called style has played a major role concerning the weight measurement reflected in the charts that man deems appropriate for the ideal body for all human beings. Man's arrogance regarding the amount of fat considered too much for human beings to carry on their bodies varies depending on the country or the year humans lived.

Today, skinny is in even if it kills you and fat is out while society eradicates all those who are over the projected normal weight. Eventually government might try to limit food and drink.

Even today companies promote hostility towards people that they feel are fat by charging double or adding additional costs. It is truly sad how money influences the world of business today instead of empathy for a human being.

I hope this chapter will open your heart to another size of life. I pray that you will share what you learn in this chapter to those that have needlessly inflicted mental pain upon another human being. One day God may bless them with understanding when they see with their heart the mental pain that they have caused others to feel.

Proverbs 14:12 Sometimes a way seems right to a man, but the end of it leads to death!

"Some stories enhance life; others degrade it. So we must be careful about the stories we tell, about the ways we define ourselves and other people." –Burton Blatt

Obesity has always been a ghost that haunts many of us at one time or another. The shackles of weight do not allow mankind to escape from people with no weight problem. I refer to people that have no problem with weight as a modern day slave master over mankind. Their tongue becomes a whip and it stings with animosity and unwillingness to offer true genuine help or sympathy.

I have always had more unwanted pounds in places than I wanted and according to the weight charts. I have been teased by boys and chastised by looks from skinny girls. I have heard the words that go unsaid upon the faces of those that are considered as normal by those charts. I have been whipped like cream by the comments of those who are brazen and bold. My heart has been defeated of joy countless times because of the sting of a tongue that its master won't tame.

James 3: 3-12

3 If we put bits into the mouths of horses to make them obey us, we also guide their whole bodies. 4 It is the same with ships: even though they are so large and driven by fierce winds, they are steered by a very small rudder wherever the pilot's inclination wishes. 5 In the same way the tongue is a small member and yet has great pretensions. Consider how small a fire can set a huge forest ablaze. 6 The tongue is also a fire. It exists among our members as a world of malice, defiling the whole body and setting the entire course of our lives on fire, itself set on fire by Gehenna. 7 For every kind of beast and bird, of reptile and sea creature, can be tamed and has been tamed by the human species, 8 but no human being can tame the tongue. It is a restless evil, full of deadly poison. 9 With it we bless the Lord and Father, and with it we curse human beings who are made in the likeness of God. 10 From the same mouth come blessing and cursing. This not need be so, my brothers. 11 Does a spring gush forth from the same opening both

pure and brackish water? 12 Can a fig tree, my brothers, produce olives, or a grapevine figs? Neither can salt water yield fresh.

Battle scars upon my stomach will never be erased from the history of my mind or body. So I have chosen to conquer this battle with the power of my mind. Are you looking at my body? Well you better get your eyes off of it. I don't view weight as other people do anymore; that is not to say that I don't have a weight problem or that the scales are my best friend. To some degree I have always felt sorry for myself concerning my weight until I met these four beautiful ladies that I will tell you about. These are only four among countless thousands upon thousands that could tell similar stories that would break your heart, that is, if you have one when it comes to obese people.

Lady One: she had the most beautiful eyes that spoke of a horror that I could only imagine. Her body would not stop gaining weight. She was trapped in her body. A medical problem was the cause for the weight gain that eventually was corrected by medicine. She didn't know one or two hundred pounds ago that medicine would have helped her. She did know though about the unruly tongues of mankind that released the most deadly, vicious venom at just the glimpse of her. Those tongues finally forced her into her home to become a shell of a human being where she found shelter and comfort from the storms that raged around her to start a process of dying. God blessed her with a friend that refused to give up on her and helped her to conquer the medical system. Lady One started a new medicine regimen that provided her with a feeling of security and a ray of hope that she could have victory in changing the person she had become. I will never forget her words to me. "I'll never be as little as you are, but I'll never be as big as I have been. At least I think I'm going to be okay as I learn to walk again, to care for myself again, and wipe my own behind again. But most of all I will make sure that my tongue

Donna Robbins

never hurts another person the way that I have been hurt."

Honesty of the Tongue

By: Donna Robbins

It is such a pretty thing
All round, fat, pink, and white
It has a job
Until it slips

Not like other parts
Such as the heart
That gushes with feelings
As one endures when it beats

Then somehow
The evil one starts to stride
Making feelings arise

Souls are flooded with anger and pride
Wondering in the mind
Why

In every thought
You must be honest and true
Your heart not bound with hatred
But filled with love

Oh yes, the tongue
It must be retrained
To sing and speak of only praise to the King
Not of malice and idle words
That will hurt or sting

Can't this tongue
Learn
Without being stung
By its brother
Another tongue

Each body part must do its own job
Without extra burden on another
So the mind will wrestle
To bridle the tongue
For this unruly part just won't learn

Lady Two: she was also homebound because of her weight. I ached with her for the pain that flooded her heart. Just going to the bathroom was a chore for her that resulted in her weeping. She affronted herself about her own weight with each movement she made. She hated herself more than anyone else ever could.

When a person can't stop eating, don't they still deserve as human beings the right to happiness, joy, and love, don't you think? Who gave any man, woman, government, society, or business the right to judge another person based on weight? Many diseases wreck our bodies and minds. This beautiful lady's disease was weight. What is yours? Is it your heart? Is it your tongue? Is it judgment? What?

_____

_____

_____

_____

_____

Matthew 4:23-25
He went around all of Galilee, teaching in their synagogues proclaiming the gospel of the kingdom, and curing every disease and illness among the people. 24 His fame spread to all of Syria, and they brought to him all who were sick with various diseases and racked with pain, those who were possessed, lunatics, and paralytics, and he cured them. 25 And great crowds from Galilee, the Decapolis, Jerusalem, and Judea, and from beyond the Jordan followed him.

Lady Three: to look at her you would not guess that the previous year she was on the heavy side; I mean that her doctor told her that she was obese. Now she was frail and weak due to a thyroid condition that had nothing to do with over eating or old age. Her clothes now hung very loosely on her body that was wasting away. Slowly, every day or two, another once, that added up to another pound that she couldn't gain back. One day as I sat on the edge of the bed with her she told me, "Enjoy good food and drink. Let others worry about your size. They have nothing more important to do with their lives that to destroy your joy. Don't take for granted that you will have tomorrow. Look at my body. How frail I have become. I would gladly trade this useless body for the one I once had. The one I learned to love, too late. I used to think about how plump I was getting. Now I can't even gain an ounce. I don't have enough strength to even fight, so that I can live. No one is fooling me. I know that with each pound I lose, I am losing my life."

Ecclesiastes 9:6-8

6 For them, love and hated and rivalry have long since perished. They will never again have part in anything that is done under the sun. 7 Go, eat your bread with joy and drink your wine with a merry heart, because it is now that God favors your works. 8 At all times let your garments be white, and spare not the perfume for your head.

Lady Four: her weight loss was due to cancer. She wasn't overly fat but because of her medical condition, I watched a perfectly normal human being that was the correct size according to those weight charts, go to a sixty-pound person. Sixty pounds when you are a child might be a healthy specimen but when it is an adult, you see a skeleton with skin holding it all together. It really is a sad sight to watch what can happen to a human being's body because of cancer. She also had to endure the facial expressions and slips of the tongue as they gasped in horror at the very sight of her without ever even acknowledging her.

On this note, I would like to address every human being that has ever let their tongue serve as a weapon towards another human being regarding weight, whether that person was slim or heavy. Are you perfect? Yes ____ or No ____

Your body may be slim or stuffed, firm and trim or somewhere in between but the size of your body can never match the love you can show a person who is not your perfect size. If you would step into their world and wear their clothes, not their shoes, then maybe you would put a lock on your lips before they have a chance to slip. Once words leave your mouth, you can't put them back in and if you could, would it truly change your heart? Please throw away your judgment and find a way to help or at least be a friend to the people that have an issue with weight. I bet that if you changed your heart you could find something nice to say to them.

Luke 6:36-38

36 Be merciful, just as [also] your Father is merciful. 37 "Stop judging and you will not be judged. Stop condemning and you will not be condemned. Forgive and you will be forgiven. 38 Give and gifts will be given to you; a good measure, packed together, shaken down, and overflowing, will be poured into your lap. For the measure with which you measure will in return be the measured out to you.'

There is one thing that people seem to forget, all of us are human beings, whatever the size of the package or how pleasant you may judge the external wrapping. Does the size of the package or the attractiveness really matter? Yes, if you are a Christmas present under a tree. All will pass through the door of death. No one will escape it or be able to find another way around it, no matter how skinny or beautiful, nor will your earthly status matter. Did you know that heaven will have an abundance of fat people who lived on earth, and hell will have more abundance of souls due to the skinny souls that roam this earth? I'm glad my home in eternity will not be judged by the size of my body, but by the contents of my heart. How will God judge you?

Those of us that don't correspond with the weight charts or I should say man's standards of comparison that we are measured by, you will have more leverage and cleavage to lose in the end.

Enjoy life in the package you are wrapped. Christmas should come every day throughout the year, not just one day, so start enjoying your own package. Take your time to unwrap the package God gave you. Start by measuring your own self-worth by God's yardstick instead of the few inches of a man/woman's tongue.

By; Heather Robbins, February 2000
Big hearts shall come beautifully wrapped without measure to the portion of the package; but loosed tongues come with small minds in an empty box.

"Every person must have a place, must be here for a special reason, or no one has a place, or no one has a special reason for being. Either everybody counts or nobody counts." -Burton Blatt

To truly understand how inhuman humans can be, read Christmas in Purgatory, A Photographic Essay on Mental Retardation by Burton Blatt and Fred Kaplan, Human Policy Press/Syracuse, New York/1974.

CHAPTER 9

B & W Bodies

This chapter sounds like a car, right. Bet you can't guess what B & W cars were parked on this lot today. I am not talking about cars though. I am talking about human beings. Can you guess what B & W stands for?

Life is more fun when you use your imagination. Without a little color in your life, it would all be black and white, much like reading a newspaper. Instead, I would rather enjoy human beings that inspire actions or feelings that produce a rainbow of color; we all do but not all realize. Life is more fun when you use your imagination. Without a little color in your life, it would all be black and white, much like reading a newspaper. Instead, I would rather enjoy human beings that inspire actions or feelings that produce a rainbow of color; we all do produce a color connected to the heart but not accepts the color that their heart produces.

This chapter is for you if you are color blind. That is if you see the influence of color incorrectly as pertaining to human beings then you are in for a treat. I am glad that God changed my blindness into caring emotions due to working with human beings. Aides that take care of human beings in hospitals, nursing homes, and private homes all across this land get to see color or the human body, even some whole bodies. Yes that hole too, no pun intended or dirty thoughts. I now understand that concept of when you have seen enough of them; they all look the same, bodies that are whole that is.

We refer to the skin on our bodies as black, white, brown, peach, et cetera. In Pre-K or Kindergarten, the children are learning about colors and skin tones. There is even that little tune that still plays in my mind from when I was a child learning about color that I even sing to my grandchildren, Jesus Loves the Little Children.

George Frederick Root composed the tune for a 1864 Civil War tune titled "Tramp, Tramp, Tramp, the Boys are Marching" and it is reported that Clare Herbert Woolston wrote the words to Jesus Loves The Little Children that was inspired by Matthew 19:14 or Matthew 18:4-6 in the New Testament.

Jesus calls the children dear,
"Come to me and never fear,
For I love the little children of the world
I will take you by the hand,
Lead you to the better land,
For I love the little children of the world."

Refrain

Jesus loves the little children,
All the children of the world.
Red and yellow, black and white,
All are precious in His sight,
Jesus loves the little children of the world.

[Alternate refrain:

Jesus died for all the children,
All the children of the world.
Red and yellow, black and white,
All are precious in His sight,
Jesus died for all the children of the world.]
Jesus is the Shepherd true,
And He'll always stand by you,
For He loves the little children of the world;
He's a Savior great and strong,
And He'll shield you from the wrong,
For He loves the little children of the world.

Refrain

I am coming, Lord, to Thee,
And Your soldier I will be,
For You love the little children of the world;
And Your cross I'll always bear,
And for You I'll do and dare,
For You love the little children of the world.

The refrain of the song is normally the part
of the song that most people sing that is well
known. I have included all three verses of the

song in view of the fact that I never knew of them until now. As well, I included the alternate refrain. After singing the whole song, I realized just how beautiful it really is.

I have failed to find human bodies that are actually only black or white, not to say they don't exist, I just haven't worked with any. In art, I learned that multicultural colors could be made by mixing different colors that could consist of two or more colors such as red, white, green, purple, blue, yellow, and browns depending on the artists choice of skin tone that they want to achieve. Look at your skin tone; you will see that it contains not just one pigment. Try to guess how many different pigments that your specific skin tone has. Do you see different colors than black or white?

When I look at other people's skin, I see different colors other than just black or white. Does this mean I am colorblind? Yes, if you see only the color of the skin and not the person under the skin. When I look at the human body, I see:

1. Sometimes only traces of what once was a productive person. I see a person who still has dignity and respect for themselves and others. Sometimes I see a shipwrecked soul fighting hard to remain young.
2. Wrinkled skin that has lost its flexibility, some only held together with strands of beauty of age, others that are cursed.
3. Some that display a look of shame or anger along with words that emphasize just how useless and vulnerable they really feel.

I had the pleasure to wash a man that had the most beautiful golden brown skin, not just the color, but also the texture that just baffled me. He was in his eighties and his skin looked and felt like a new born baby. Yes, there were wrinkles, but few and far between. At first, he thought I was mysteriously strange and too curious. I could not stop touching and exploring his body. Don't get any funny ideas. Stop your imaginations from running wild at this point even if you are having fun at my expense.

I kept asking him questions and commenting how youthful his skin looked. He smiled at me with eyes of wisdom and truth. He was just as amazed at me for the genuine interest I had in his skin. He was very kind to share his secret, pure virgin olive oil. He stated very boldly, "In the Bible it states that it was given to the people to use all those years ago, then it is good enough for me too." He was just as amazed to learn that I loved the Lord and new of His word, the Bible too.

Psalms 104:15 and wine to gladden our hearts, Oil to make our faces gleam, food to build our strength.

Well, I don't know how you see the color of skin, but the color of this man's skin shouted vitality from the living God, Jehovah, Lord, and Savior. I started using olive oil and over the years even learned how to infuse it with lavender that I grow in the garden. I hope that in years to come my skin will look as youthful as his when I become his age.

Through him I learned a lot about B & W bodies and all the other colors in-between over the next few months. We respected each other as unique individuals that God had created to show each other the path of understanding for not just color but as a man and woman and as children of God. Has this changed your vision concerning color? _____

Please try this test but with a friend first. Then if you find the courage to try this in the true meaning that it is meant for, put on a blindfold and walk down Main Street of your hometown. Just remember you may need help if you still see only black or white after this test since this test will show you the true color of skin of your heart.

Color Test

One way to test yourself:

Put on a blindfold.

Talk to a stranger.

Now ask that stranger to let you touch their face.

If they say yes, explore the structure of their face such as their eyes, cheekbones, nose, and chin. Do you feel smooth or rough skin?

_____

What are you thinking?

_____

_____

_____

What can you tell about that person from the color test by just feeling their face?

_____

_____

_____

What color was this person's skin?

_____

Remember B & W bodies are rare to non-existent, but in the mind of mankind, color does exist with equally out of control spectrums from all races as they deem that they are more important than the next human being. You now have experienced the true color of a human's skin and the source from within that judges. Did it come from a heart of compassion or a heart of contempt? When we judge our own heart, we gain knowledge in understanding the truth of color from the spectrum of God's paint brushes. Was it not God Himself who created man in His own image, not color?

Genesis 1:26-28 & 2:7

26 Then God said, "Let us make man in our image, after our likeness: Let them have dominion over the fish of the sea, the birds of the air, and the cattle, and over all the wild animals and the creatures that crawl on the ground." 27 God created man in his image, in the divine image he created them; male and female he created them. 28 God blessed them, saying to them: "Be fruitful and multiply, fill

the earth and subdue it. Have dominion over the fish of the sea the birds of the air, and all the living things that move on the earth."

2:7 then the Lord God formed man out of the clay of the ground, and blew into his nostrils the breath of life, and so man became a living being.

My sunglasses will darken in the sunlight
But what causes my eyes to strain
My fear darkens the light that I need to see with
That leads my soul to righteousness
My acquiescence to color
Keeps me blinded to the truth - Donna Robbins,
February 2000

CHAPTER 10

ABC's of Dignity

Just because you are older doesn't mean that you
will lose your dignity. How would you use your
imagination to maintain your dignity in the eyes
of another human being? I am going to asking
you to try on a pair of shoes. They are a pair of
brown leather sandals size eight, so worn out
that they may fall apart with the next step that
you take, but they are also the only shoes you
own. I am asking you to imagine that you are a
ninety-four year-old woman; some moments of
time escape you, like what you ate for breakfast,
but you are still very alert for this age. Some
moments of time escape you, like what you
ate for breakfast. On the other hand, I mean
foot, you remember quite well the fear that over
took you fifteen years ago when your husband
died leaving you alone. Your days and nights
no longer matter since you have outlived your
spouse and friends. Your vision has become

clouded, furnishing only shades of gray that offer only incomplete pictures for you to view. Time is only the sound that the clock makes.

You are sitting in your favorite chair when you feel a warm sensation between your legs. You realize that you just urinated in your underpants. It was that reoccurring dream that you were on the commode when you realize that you are still in your chair. You stand to your feet and begin to remove the wet underpants when it becomes clear to you that you are not alone in the room. You are aware that someone has invaded your space; you hesitate till you hear the sound of the person's voice that is in the room with you. You recognize the owner of the voice; it brings calmness after being startled. You finish removing the wet underpants with your friend's help. Then you hear your friend ask a dreaded question that floods your mind with despising thoughts, how dare she ask such a question. You try to avoid answering that question and then she asks the question again, "Why did you pee in your pants?"

Use your imagination to come up with an answer for this question before reading how she saved her dignity when this aide, me did not think before she asked such a question.

_____

_____

_____

_____

_____

I hope your imagination was as good as hers. She gave losing control of your bladder a new meaning. In her mind, she maintained her dignity as she briefly told this story. "I took a lobster out of the freezer and forgot I left it in my chair. I didn't realize it had thawed out when I sat on it."

My Brother

By: Donna Robbins

My brother sees my sorrow
My Jesus sees my pain

My brother speaks to entrap me
My Jesus releases all that hurts my heart
Which my brother cannot do

My brother toils and spins a trap to snare my
soul
My Jesus speaks to my heart
And then opens the eyes to my soul

My brother, I wish I could trust
My Jesus, I render my life

My brother thinks he knows what is best for me
As if I were still a child

My Lord Jesus Christ
Gives me room to spread my wings and fly
Then He pulls the strings to my heart
And keeps me in line

My brother try's to cut the strings
That he knows will hold my dignity intact
As I desire to remain a man/woman
Not a child of the world but of God

My Lord Jesus Christ, my savior,
Watches me with delight
Till I grow closer to him

The definition of DIGNITY, according to the Encarta online Dictionary goes something like this:

Worth and merit, implies conduct in keeping with one's position or ones self-respect.

1. Worthiness: I say don't take your loves ones for granted.
   1 Peter 2:17, Give honor to all, love the community, fear God, honor the king.

2. Honor: Someone else's pain can be yours too. How you treat another person can heel or destroy what is left in the last stages of their life. Life can be very fragile so handle with care.
   Proverbs 22:4, The reward of humility and fear of the Lord is riches, honor and life.

3. How important is honor? You are born naked, you will leave in clothing, and the only thing you will take with you is your personal memories of how you lived your life upon this earth. Wonder why you never see a U-Haul trailer behind a hearse?

   Job 1:21, and said, "Naked I came forth from my mother's womb, and naked shall I go back again. The Lord gave and the Lord has taken away; blessed be the name of the Lord."

4. A title: Sometimes titles grant special privileges or things that a person can cherish always. Don't ask why, just give thanks you have them.

   Ephesians 5:20, giving thanks always and for everything in the name of our Lord Jesus Christ to God the Father.

5. Great value: The most important thing in life is not what you have but how in the end you let them go.

Proverbs 22:1, A good name is more desirable that great riches, and high esteem, than gold and silver.

6. Dignity: When all is said and done, what remains a heart full of memories or a treasure chest full of pain?
Matthew 6:21 For where your treasure is, there also will your heart be.

7. Worship: The greatest treasures you gain on earth are not made of metal, wood, or gold, but only one ingredient, the love you've given as it comes back tenfold.
Leviticus 19:31 "Do not go to mediums or consult fortune tellers, for you will be defiled by them. I, the LORD, am you God.

It is time that we take inventory of what we treasure. What returns will come from the treasures you think you own?

_____

_____

_____

Do you think these returns will be enough for you until your last breath?

_____

_____

_____

1st Timothy 6:7, For we brought nothing into the world, just as we shall not be able to take anything out of it.

The biggest return (treasure) that I have received for services rendered on behalf of my King came on the wings of a prayer while working with this very sweet human being named Barbara. This treasure will unfold in the next story.

Barbara was a beautiful client and her spirit was pure. She was sixty-five years old or young. Barbara was a slender woman. Her frail body revealed that she also knew the stranger named Cancer, who was a resident in her body. She had been battling this stranger for five years. She told me once that she wished she had her mother's genes instead of her father's. I asked her why and she told me that her mother was still running her own business and her father died years ago from cancer.

We became very close in a very short period. We spent two weeks together, but we shared out entire lives, our faith, our love for Jesus Christ, and compassion for each other as sisters in Christ. She could have been my mother. I poured my love into her through my hands as I massaged her much like I did my own grandmother each time I saw her. I opened my heart and I heard her pain. Our last day together she went from being alert to extreme pain that consumed all her emotions; my last words as she laid weak and broken were, "When you get to heaven tell Jesus I said hello. Send me a sign. I love you." She answered, "Okay, I love you too."

This day was like all the other days that we had shared with each other but I knew in my heart she meant it. Barbara knew how she had touched my heart in just the past few weeks. See, each day as I started to leave Barbara's house I would tell her, "If you get to heaven before I do tell Jesus to come tell me hello" and she would smile and answer back, "If you get to heaven before I do you tell Jesus to come get me that I am ready to go home."

At the foot of Barbara's bed hung a picture roughly three feet wide by six feet in height of Jesus with the words, "JESUS I TRUST IN YOU" written across the bottom. Being that I was Catholic, I assume she thought that I knew about the picture and what it represented. She told me that the picture gave her inner peace to gaze upon it as she lay there in bed. She kept telling me that she was just passing time until Jesus came to take her home.

April 30, 2000 I attended my first sunrise service since my family moved to Niagara Falls, New York from Conway South Carolina in 1990. Heather and Sarah were papergirls for the Niagara Gazette and after we delivered the paper on this particular morning, we rushed to the sunrise service on Goat Island down by the Falls. I had promised the girls that after the sunrise service, we would go home and they could go back to bed. But as I left the Island, it was like someone else was driving the car. Deep down inside of me there was this feeling that I had to go to our church for Mass. After lots of protest from the girls, we went inside the church. As others came into the church, Heather elbowed me and pointed to our wet pants and shoes due to the morning dew from the sunrise service. See I was raised that you dressed your best to go to God's house. No pants. My words were honest and true as I told Heather, "We got up early and dressed our hearts today for the Lord, so I don't think He will mind if we wear pants for just this Sunday."

After mass, the Deacon brought out a big picture and placed it on an easel near the church altar. He invited everyone to stay as he would be explaining and leading the Divine Mercy prayer. I physically could not move out of the seat. Both girls elbowed me and said, "You promised we would go home." I could only assure them that there had to be a reason for us to stay. Then Heather went and got the Divine Mercy booklet for us to pray from.

After the Deacon gave a little history about the picture, everyone kneeled and began praying the Divine Mercy Prayer on Rosary beads. As I kneeled there, I heard a voice call my name; I looked around and did not see anyone that was not praying. I started praying again. I heard my name again. I looked at Heather and Sarah to see if they were calling me but they both were reading from the booklet. So I started praying the Divine Mercy prayer again. I heard my name again. This time the voice spoke with authority "HELLO DONNA." I looked up. Beside the picture was a cloud like mist that was in the shape of Jesus that was in the Divine Mercy picture. I then realized that the picture in the church was also the same picture that hung at the foot of Barbara's bed. I was speechless.

Barbara had died a few days before that Easter of 2000. She kept her promise. Jesus, my Lord and Savior came that morning of April 30, 2000 just to tell me hello. This was my first encounter with the true meaning of The Divine Mercy. If you are reading this, I would like to encourage you to read the Diary of Saint Maria Faustina Kowalska, Divine Mercy in my Soul.

The next year I visited my mother in S.C. She showed me a picture that one of her friend's daughters had taken inside of an airplane during a lighting storm. In the picture, there is a cloud that is in the shape of Jesus of the Divine Mercy picture that looked like the form of mist that spoke to me in church that Easter morning. I can't describe in words how much these pictures look alike when placed side by side nor how they speak to the heart of those who look at them.

CHAPTER 11

End of the Beginning

Several years later, I had to return to the nursing home setting again because my husband's job ended and we needed money to survive in this world. After resigning from my first nursing home job, I wandered away from my faith after the seeds of resentment that I never noticed had taken hold. Then God blessed me as I returned to work and provided my heart with compassion again. As I walked down that old familiar road of judgment, I prayed that the seeds in my spiritual life called faith, hope, and charity that had been planted long ago would regenerate my spiritual journey forward.

1st Timothy 6: 10 For the love of money is the root of all evils, and some people in their desire for it have strayed from the faith and have pierced themselves with many pains.

One particular night in the nursing home, those seeds did take root and sprouted into a new direction, as a pair of blue eyes stared at me. Those blue eyes were deadlocked on every movement that I made. I could feel those blue eyes penetrating my very soul. Never to this day have I ever encountered another pair of blue eyes that spoke with so much love, without speaking, as those, other than my dad's.

Eyes of Blue

By: Donna Robbins-November 1992

Eyes as blue as the clouds up above
A silver lining they behold

Like stars they dance before my King
As majestic rare jewels
Concealed inside of their own power
An inspiration of joy

Deep as the oceans
Prosperous beyond their wildest dreams

Adorned with love

Just look inside of them
What beauty you will see that
God so elegantly dressed to last through the
years
So forgive me as I stare
For the blessings I find in those eyes of blue
Carry me back to childhood
When I had eyes of royal blue too
As we await the day that eyes of royal blues
Will dance before their Heavenly King

Blue eye's body (patient in nursing home) had
returned to a fetal position that rendered her
crippled, not able to even sit up in a chair. Her
voice no longer heard by anyone on earth, but
her blue eyes told you everything, especially if
she chose to make you aware that she existed.
I had finished rotating her from side to side
to prevent bed sores and checked her bottom
for wetness. Kind of sounds like I'm grilling
chicken, beef, turkey, or pork, hum? If you
lose your sense of humor in the nursing home

setting your protein, (humor) quickly cooks to a well-done status. I always talked to blue eyes upon entering her room and believed within my heart that she could hear me even though she never spoke a word about whatever subject matter I was babbling about. Sometimes I knew that she was smiling just by the look in her eyes.

That day as I approached the door of the room and turned back to say good bye and that I would see her in a little while like I always did, those words did not come this time. Instead, when I looked in her blue eyes they spoke to me. What they said I couldn't understand, but I knew she was communicating something. I walked over to the bed and gently pushed her hair away from her face so that I could see her blue eyes more clearly. The words I spoke were simple, "I wonder if you are someone's grandmother. I bet if you were given a chance you would be a grand old light house to them too," even though I never heard of anyone visiting blue eyes.

I thought I saw a glimpse of sunshine dance in her eyes. I thought she smiled. When I stepped away from the bed, I felt that ray of sunshine. There was a glow covering both of us on this dark night. It was a feeling of warmth that touched and filled every inch of our body's inside and out. So much love and peace rushed over me. I found myself being held in a tender embrace.

I finally looked upward from where this source of peace was coming from. I could only see a bright light. From this light, I felt my great-grandmother's presence. At least that's who I felt that it was in my heart because I could feel her arms around me, holding me once again. In retrospect, it could have been Jesus.

While I continued looking upwards, I felt tears run down my face. I heard myself speak from a humbled heart, "I hope you are proud of me great-grandma." When I looked back at those blue eyes, they were unquestionably smiling back at me. The ray of golden light began to grow dim and I remembered my own great-grandmother's words of wisdom, which she quite often shared with me as they came back through the corridors of my mind: "Don't let the sun go down on your anger." Later in life I realized her wisdom was biblical.

Ephesians 4:26, Be angry but do not sin; do not let the sun go down on your anger,"

My grandmother, another beautiful lady, gave unconditional love to her children and grandchildren. She left behind a legacy of her faith, which continues to seed the future generations. I had the honor and privilege to have been a recipient of those seeds of wisdom, knowledge, and love that she had for her God, which is my God too. God blessed me with a great-grandmother, a grandmother, and a mother that molded my life to love God. They truly were and are the lighthouses that God sent to keep my light burning until I would one day grow to love Him as much as they did in their lifetimes and to share these seeds with my own children and grandchildren who have graced my life and prayerfully other generations as well. Their love was unconditional as it flowed from God that radiates through the words of this poem that I wrote for my grandmother one Christmas after moving to NY. We were broke as usual and I wrote this poem, framed it in a paper frame, and glued gold tinsel around the outer edge then sent it to her. My husband a few years later thought he would surprise me and entered it into a poetry contest online and it was published, which can be found on line by typing in, The Grand Old Light House by Donna Robbins.

That Grand Old Light House

By: Donna Robbins-Christmas 1992

As I view the subsistence of my life
A melody appears
To the reflections of a child and the sounds of time
Building to a place that I've become

A face with tiny wrinkles
The hair a tent of gray
Her eyes hold a gleam
To help a dreamer on their way
My Grand Old Light House
To this day

A hand firm but filled with love a child could
understand
A gentleness of spirit to urge you into another
day
My first glimpse of
JESUS
In my
Grand Old Light House
To this day

The pains of a child become so real
As I look back through those eyes
To see how she wished to make all the hurt stop
The point reached between Grandmother and
child
The place where each knows to look
At the peak of dawn

And
The destination she would choose
For each of her bundles of delight
Grandmother
You are that
Grand Old Light House
In my life

(When my grandmother passed away, I rewrote
this poem to include all her grand, great-grand,
and great-great-grandchildren and read it at her
funeral.)

Shortly after this encounter with blue eyes in the
nursing home I experienced a great saddening
to my soul. It concerned a gentleman that was
not able to get out of bed. He could talk, but
chose not to. When trying to roll him over to
clean his bottom he would become stiff and use
his arms to push himself backwards creating
hardship for the aide when trying to care for
him. Upon bathing him that evening I felt
another kindred spirit, my grandfather, and for
a moment I remembered a game of checkers

that I played with him as a child; grandfather said, "Being poor isn't anything to be ashamed of Sue. Poor people are closer to God." I asked him why. He lowered his eyes to the bottle caps that we were playing with on top of a homemade checkerboard and said, "Because we aren't born to be kings on this earth. You got to be clever until the real King comes back, just like in this game, you have to outsmart the other man if you're going to be the king and take the other persons checker. The riches that you will want in the future will only come through hard work and the sweat of your brow. In life my sweetheart, always let Jesus be your King." I jumped his last king and won the game. "You mean like this grandfather," and I saw him smile, a smile that graced my own father's lips through the years. Actually, we were very poor but I never truly knew that until I became an adult

As I look back, both of them seemed to have carried so much pain inside. I became very aware with this thought, that wherever my grandfather was he could be in pain and agony. This feeling made me tremble with fear for what I sensed, as I looked into this patient's eyes and for the first time I noticed, he was in agony and great despair. I have often wondered if that man had chosen to speak, what would he have said that day besides what his face revealed. Many times since that day, I have wished that I had asked him this question, do you know Jesus?

The Secret

By: John C. Robbins

The secret to growing as God's child
Is
When you read or hear God's word
Apply all of what you read or heard
Only to your own self
Don't
Fall trap to fitting God's message
Into someone else's spiritual needs
First
Seek and keep yourself without sin

Without judgment
Or condemnation
Then
Do God's will
Pray
And let God
Handle and guide
The spiritual help of others

In the nursing home death always seemed to come when we least expected, even though we knew that it was always right around the corner. Death is a subject that brings many different emotions such as joy, peace, loss, anger, fright, finality, loneliness, and many other misunderstood feelings until you experience death, be it a loved one or friend.

The first night of November, we lost a lovely lady to our comrade of Death who often walked the halls following us. I did not get to see this lady's death when the comrade of Death took her, but I spoke to her aide that was with her and the following is the aide's version of what she experienced with this lady in those final seconds. The aide was brushing this lady's (patient) hair. The Lady was looking into the mirror that she held in her hand. The aide saw the lady's smile in the mirror's reflection and thought that she saw stars twinkling in this lady's eyes. The aide said, "You would have thought she saw her first love again. There was a glow in the mirror which I thought was the reflection from the light in the room" as she told me and the other aides. I knew in my soul that it wasn't the light in the room that she saw; it was lights from Heaven.

On the second night of November, our comrade of Death came again. This time I will agree, death can be horrible. I was on my scheduled hall of the nursing home wing when the Code Blue came across the intercom. As I ran out into the hall, I saw the blue code light flashing in the hallway and followed it to the patient's room, which was one of mine. As I entered the room, another aide appeared in the doorway behind me. The nurse was on top of the patient in the

Donna Robbins

bed trying desperately to pull her forward into
a sitting position. The nurse told us to get up on
the bed and help pull her (patient) forward. I can
still here the nurse's words, "We are losing her!"
You could hear the fear that was in the nurse's
voice as she repeated, "arm in arm ladies, arm
in arm." Facing the patient I slipped my left arm
underneath the patient's arm and the other aide
slipped her right arm under the patient's arm
and we began pulling her forward; as we pulled
forward this elderly patient pushed backwards
with such force that the two of us could not
hold her in an upright sitting position. It seemed
as if the patient was trying to get away from
something. The other aide and I locked eyes
and we looked towards the head of the bed. We
both reached for the top of the mattress behind
the patient's head to help pull her forward. I will
never forget the look on this patient's face as
she was face to face with the comrade of Death.
Both I and the other aide were only inches from
this patient's face. The patient's eyes started to
bulge and the sclera (white part) of her eye turn
red, like blood overflowing the banks of a river.

160

The iris and pupil part of her eyes resembled large chunks of black coal. I did not realize what she was seeing at that moment just seconds from death's door, but the look in her eyes let us know there was more happening than we were aware of. I was frightened from the look of fear that gripped her face as the comrade of Death began to snatch her from us.

The nurse once again began yelling, "We're losing her." My arm was still wrapped underneath the patient's arm when I felt the warmth leaving her body, being replaced with coolness as the sound of her final breath echoed in the room. I never knew that death's touch was so quick to rob the body of warmth. How naive this southern girl was in the department of life and death as I observed that look of fright that never left her (patient) face until I closed her eyes and mouth from the sting of death.

That's when I noticed that same blood red color had invaded the inside of her tiny pink mouth as well.

I had the honor of tending to the details of preparing the body for the coroner that our comrade of death left behind. The other aide offered to help and I gladly accepted. The other aide stayed only a few minutes before she turned to me and said, "I can't" and she then left the room. I stood there alone, with the corpse. I began to tremble with the unusual coldness that filled the room.

I don't know why I stayed; maybe I was trying to remember all the details. The events kept playing repeatedly in my mind as I remembered looking into this patient's eyes. I was numb from the coldness of the room. I checked the thermostat and knew that the cold wasn't from lack of heat as it flowed from the heating vents. Then suddenly a different aide came busting through the door and announced she was there to help me finish since I was taking so long. I did feel a sigh of relief even though she was not friendly. The aide walked over to the closet, picked up a washcloth and walked back towards the body. She starred at the corpse for what seemed like an eternity and then looked me straight in the eyes and said, "Something's not right here. It is too cold in here. Something's not right. There is something in this room besides us." Then she dropped the washcloth on the foot of the bed, turned to me and said, "I am out of here." I finished the details of tending to the body after death had taken her life and then left the room. When I left the room, the other aides just stared at me, mumbled something to each other, and walked away. Neither I nor the other two aides could explain to the nurse or the other aides the feeling of eeriness in this particular room nor how it turned as cold as the weather outside, especially when the nursing home was always so hot.

After my shift that night, I tried to explain to my husband the events that had occurred and the look that seemed to be glued on the patient's face even after death. This look never left my memory and over the next few days that look produced, a poem that explained what this woman had experienced in my opinion. I tried to put myself into her shoes to comprehend the event and that's as far as I ever want to walk in her shoes or anyone else's. As I wrote concerning these events again, I still see her face and those eyes that screamed of horror and my heart is already racing.

Book of Wisdom 1:12
Court not death by your erring way of life, nor draw to yourselves destruction by the works of your hands.

Book of Wisdom 2: 23-24
For God formed man to be imperishable; the image of his own nature he made him. But by the envy of the devil, death entered the world, and they who are in his possession experience it.

DEATH

By: Donna Robbins

From out of the pits of hell I see
Satan coming after me
For what I put off I now will endure

My time for death has come at last
Can I fight it
I'm not for sure

What thoughts can be more unpleasant than
these
You think you're something
Only to find

Your heart has stop
Your soul begins rise
Leaving your body behind

Are you ready
Surprise

And end we all must face
Some will be old full and full of grace
Others young life unknown
Where or when
You are not told
How will your soul be sold

Donna Robbins

Be ready
Not in doubt
As you travel to the other side
You may pay a much greater toll
Depending on which road you now must take

For shall you see
A band of angels and Jesus' grace
Or
The pits of Hell and Satan's face

Book of Wisdom 3: 1 But the souls of the just are in the hand of God, and no torment shall touch them.

As America continues to remove God from our schools, public places, government, and even in some churches in America, people have become so dense concerning God in their lives. It seems we no longer wish to fight for the true freedom; the freedom to worship God here in America. The strong in spirit that fight for spiritual equality do not win all spiritual battles for freedom but they do prevent total destruction even when their beliefs are based on the fact that God should have no effect in the lives of mankind. As atheists or other religions push God out of the social mainstream, is it the fulfilling of Christ's return? Will God walk or send his angels to walk with you that last mile of the journey to your eternal home or will you see Satan and his demons at deaths door? We have become entangled in a spiritual net designed by Satan that traps the minds spiritual power; therefore leaving us void of the true meaning of why we were given life in the first place.

Book of Revelations 1:4-8

John, to the seven churches in Asia: grace to you and peace from him who is and who was and who is to come, and from the seven spirits before his throne, 5 and from Jesus Christ, the faithful witness, the firstborn of the dead, and the ruler of the kings of the earth. To him who loves us and has freed us from our sins by his blood, 6 who has made us into a kingdom, priests for his God and Father, to him be glory and power forever (and ever). Amen. 7 Behold, he is coming amid the clouds, and every eye will see him, even those who pierced him. All the people of the earth will lament him. Yes, Amen. 8 "I am the Alpha and the Omega," says the Lord God, "the one who is and who was and who is to come, the Almighty."

Where does God fit into your life? Do you have Him on a shelf or is He completely out of your life? Does He guide your ship to safe harbors or do you only call upon His name when you're battling the storms of life? Will He be waiting for you at the end of your life's journey or will you meet Satan who will walk you to a place you thought you would not go? Did you listen to the small still voice that disturbed your thoughts from time to time? Use the following space to write down your walk with God. Please be honest, your soul depends on it.

Knock Knock

Who's there?

Who?

WHEN SOMETHING SWEET IS DIPPED INTO SOMETHING SWEETER THEY BECOME BITTER IN THE MOUTH OF THE WORLD

There are numerous feelings about death that human beings experience as I said earlier but I am only going to touch on two types:

<u>First type of death most consider normal</u>: a person is waiting to walk through deaths door at the end of their journey in life. They are ready to embrace death, even welcome it. Most people understand this feeling as they watch their loved ones struggling to maintain balance in the bout of old age or terminal illness as the person tries to gracefully put closure to their lives. Sometimes death is a relief to the family, this is not said to be cruel. The family knows that their loved one has experienced a beginning, middle, and now they are waiting for the end.

<u>Second type of death that is offensive to most:</u> death comes suddenly and is unexpected. Death was the last thing you believed could or would happen to you, someone you love, or someone you know. When this happens, death just seems to rip out your inner self stability. These deaths leave you with a thousand questions and raw emotions; after all, we live contrary to the fact that we will die before we become old? What age is old, or the life span of a human being and by whose standards; man considers 65 +, God's word 120.

DEATH

By Donna Robbins

You say they're gone home
A place beyond the stars

What about my home
As I am here alone

No one left to wipe the tears
Or lock the doors

To shut off the last burning light
Or wake with you at dawns first light

One less plate, glass, and fork
One lonelier day to bear

No one to watch the family grow old with

HELP ME LORD

Help me Lord explain to the small ones

Because I can't find the words
To explain to them
Why their daddy's gone home

A place beyond the stars
To await for me and them

This next story is very dear to my heart. It was
the last time my heart was allowed to speak

to my earthly father before he died. I am so grateful that my Heavenly Father granted us this opportunity. On January 20, 1997, my earthly father was taken from this earth at an early age of 58. Sunday morning, January 19, 1997 started out just like other past Sunday mornings when on call; it was cold and snowy in the north. I was off to another Hospice case and as always, you never knew how long they would be here on earth. I had come to terms with the fact that you never knew what would happen in a two hour time frame, which was usually the allotted time for each patient in home health care. The client that I saw this day was waiting for death and praying that it would come quickly. Each day I knew death would come to her to door and I prayed I wasn't there. What I didn't know was just how close death was to my own family's door as gloom overshadowed my emotions.

When I returned home that morning from this Hospice case, my husband and my two daughters met me at the front door. I could tell by the look on their faces something was wrong. Before I could take off my coat, John was asking me to sit down because he had some bad news, never a good sign. My first thoughts were, something had happened to Jazzmen, our dog. I started walking to the back door of our home when John took hold of my arm; I asked, "Is Jazzmen dead?" He said very slowly, "Donna it's not Jazz, it's your dad. Will you please sit down?"

Mentally, I was too scared to sit down. I did not want to hear any more of what he was going to say. I refused to sit down, thinking that whatever it was that he was going to tell me would not be true if I did not hear it. I didn't like the sound that was in John's voice, it made what I was about to be told too final. I went numb and I ran to the phone. If I reacted fast enough I could stop what was happening. John's words played over and over in my thoughts as I faintly remembered dialing the number to the hospital, "Donna your dad has had a heart attack, they don't know if he will live." Suddenly my thoughts were interrupted as a strange voice answered the phone, even though I recognized that it was my aunt's voice.

My mother always called me by Sue, my middle name. I heard my mother's voice over the phone in the background asking if it was me. Once my mother got to the phone she said, "Sue it's not good. You need to come." I told her I would get there as fast as I could. I hung up the phone and started calling the airlines and bus stations only to find out that nothing was leaving Niagara Falls or Buffalo until Monday morning. Frustration started to set in as none of the plans that I was trying to make were working out. Thank goodness that my brain was working because my heart was breaking and raw emotions were running my self-control. It is not easy to prepare to walk away from your children and husband with no knowledge of when you will return. At the same time, you know that you need to be by your father's side. Fear floods your heart, not knowing when or if death will knock on his door. You only know that you have to remain strong so that you can give support to your mother and family.

Early Monday morning I realized that I could not get to SC right away. I finally made my body lay down. I was hoping that sleep would take away my raw emotions when suddenly guilt rushed over me. All the things that I had said or done to hurt or failed to say or do before this moment came to mind. I had taken for granted that my father would always be here on earth. As I lay waiting for sleep or daylight, which ever would come first, I tried to remember my father's face. Those were my last thoughts as sleep came. I began to dream, then I suddenly walked into the ICU at the hospital where my father lay on a stretcher with one arm hanging off that I placed across his chest and kissed his face, then said, "Daddy I'm here." As I looked into his face, I realized that a bright light, much brighter than the sun began to shine underneath my father as he laid on that stretcher. His body started to rise and it had changed. He was transparent as I viewed the light that shown through him.

Donna Robbins

Shadow of a human form but I knew it was still my father. The light was no longer blinding, as it became a soft glow with white and pale shades of blue as his transforming body lingered just above the floor in front of me.

As my father stood in front of me floating in air, he became a translucent light show. I couldn't tell where my father's body stopped and the light began. Suddenly hands appeared; they were trying to grab hold of my father's body. Don't ask how I knew, but I knew the hands belonged to Satan. I grabbed hold of my father just above his knees and began to pray as my father's body was rising upwards. I awoke in my bed in a sitting position as sweat poured from every inch of my body. I lay back down in the bed. As my head once again rested on my pillow, confusion and fright flooded my soul. I knew I had to pray, not that the Lord wouldn't take my father, but not to take him until all was right. What was right? What was wrong? I dared not to ask. I just knew that was the prayer that I needed to pray. I closed my eyes and prayed like I never prayed before and as I prayed I realized that I was back in the ICU room again. This time I saw that Satan did not have a hold of my father, but that he was desperately trying to obtain a hold on him.

I became aware of another person, spirit, or presence in the room over in the left hand corner of the ICU room. I looked up and the four of us, my father, Satan, myself, and the one unidentified being went through the ceiling. I awoke, looked up at the clock, 5:26 am. Ten minutes later, the phone rang. I turned to John and said, "Daddy's gone." John asked me then how did I know. As I answered the phone my mother confirmed what I knew, my father was gone. Another soul lost to the comrade of death. I did not want to admit that my father's life had ended on earth but I could comprehend that the end of life was the beginning of a new and different one.

Book of Wisdom 3:1 But the souls of the just are in the hand of God, and no torment shall touch them.

177

We arranged time off with our jobs and school on that Monday morning and then we headed to South Carolina for my father's funeral. After we arrived in SC, the first few days were consumed with funeral arrangements and then the funeral, not for me to say good bye but for the rest of the family to say good bye.

A week passed before my mother and I found time to be alone and talk. I shared with her my last good bye with daddy. I approached the table where he laid, his same right arm hanging off the table that was also hanging off the stretcher in the ICU. Both times I placed his arm across his chest and kissed his face. As I began to describe the ICU room where my father had laid on the stretcher, my mother began to cry. I then told her how the outside wall of the ICU room consisted mostly of windows from about waist high off the floor reaching to the ceiling of the room and I described how the door in the room opened to the nurse's station that was directly across from his room. Oh, yes, and what the ceiling tiles looked like. When I had finished, I took her in my arms and held her until she stopped crying. She then replied, "You are right in all of these details." The next week my mother took me to the hospital where we visited the ICU room from the outside courtyard where my father had died. This part of the hospital was a new addition to the existing hospital that only recently had opened; I had never seen nor heard about this new wing of the ICU until the morning of January, Nineteen Hundred and Ninety Seven. The last piece of the puzzle came together when the death certificate came for my father, the time of death was one minute before I awoke and looked at my clock; just one minute difference.

I know with all my heart that my dad and I were granted one last chance to say our final good bye until we meet again. I do not know why I was granted this opportunity and have stopped asking God why. I now cherish the experience and pass the memories on to my own sweet children and anyone else who cares to listen. I pray unendingly that my dear Lord will please grant me this wish, don't let me leave this world

Donna Robbins

without telling my husband and my own dear children and grandchildren good bye, and that I love them. Sometimes in the rush of the day or in the heat of the argument we sometimes forget to stop and say to our loved ones, "I LOVE YOU."

Ecclesiastes 12: 6-8
Before the silver cord is snapped and the golden bowl is broken, And the pitcher is shattered at the spring, and the broken pulley falls into the well, And the dust returns to the earth as it once was, and the life breath returns to God who gave it. Vanity of vanities, says Qoheleth, all things are vanity.

The most loving memory that I have left of my father's death was this dream, which I will cherish until I die because it was my Heavenly Father who granted this final good bye between us. My earthly father and I shared a bond that joined out hearts with an unspoken love.

Matthew 6: 21 For where your treasure is, there also will your heart be.

LITTLE GARDEN

By: Donna Robbins

I thought my garden (SPIRIT) was beautiful
It looked as if I was off to a great start
I toiled the ground (FAITH)
Put in new fertilizer (WISDOM)
And planted seeds (HOPE)
I walked the floors for days, weeks
Nothing seemed to be growing (ME)
I had not picked up another rake (BIBLE)
Or turned the ground (FAITH)
Just sitting and waiting
I finally put it on the back burner out of my mind
Then the neighbor who gave me the seeds (HOPE)
Asked how my garden (SPIRIT)
Was growing (ME)
The preacher who helped pick out the best fertilizer (WISDOM)
Asked to look at my little garden (SPIRIT)
I felt this pain of sadness deep within
As I looked at my little garden (SPIRIT)

From within

All I could do was cry and ask why

Then one day I turned over the cornerstone (JESUS)

At the edge of my little garden (SPIRIT)

And behold there were little green shoots (A HOPE OF NEW FAITH)

The weather turned warm

The sun shined brighter

And a sprinkle of rain (ALL GOD) appeared

I got off my feet onto my knees

I pulled every weed (DEVIL)

Raked (READ THE BIBLE)

And fertilized (APPLIED WISDOM)

To every plant (CHARITY)

In that ground (MY FAITH)

The next thing I knew my garden (SPIRIT)

Was greener and growing faster than I could conceive

I was so happy and excited

Then serenity settled in and

I went back to my old ways

I didn't toil the ground (MY FAITH)

Rake (READ THE BIBLE)

Or apply fertilizer (WISDOM OF GOD)
Then terrible storms (PROBLEMS)
Came and wrecked my little garden (SPIRIT)
I thought what is the use in replanting this garden (SPIRIT)
Somewhere from within the soil (SOUL)
A small voice (GOD)
Said if you don't replant your little garden (SPIRIT)
You will have no fruit (PIECE OF HEAVEN)
To feed yourself
This really bothered me
I got back on my knees in my little garden (SPIRIT)
And changed my ways
Instead of burning out my joy (SALVATION)
I let my little garden (SPIRIT)
Grow as the garden of my faith did
As my little garden (SPIRIT)
Comes to an end one day, after its season (MY LIFE)
On earth, I will have more fruits (PIECES OF HEAVEN)
Than I can enjoy

CHAPTER 12

The Darkest Hour

Book of Wisdom 2: 23, 24

23 For God formed man to be imperishable; the image of his own nature he made him. 24 But by the envy of the devil, death entered the world, and they who are in his possession experience it.

Death can be a very strange bedfellow, don't you think; my first encounter with this quietus was as a child when my great-grandfather who had been bed ridden for years died. Later in life, I came to know the meaning behind the term bed ridded. As a child, I thought it meant that he rode his bed. He was always on his bed, which was extremely high or maybe it was high because I was small and always needed help to get up there to sit and talk with him. All the grand and great-grandchildren begged to sit on his bed because he had this red and gray sock monkey that was as large as us children or so it seemed. Today every time I see a sock monkey I think of my great-grandfather; they went together just like peanut butter and jelly. It's funny how we dismiss the significance of time and events that affected aspects of our lives.

I remember the last time I saw my great-grand father. The trip to his house started out different than all the other times that we had visited; my parents acted strange, their temperament was different and my mother kept wiping her eyes. As a child, I did not understand why my parents and grand-parents, and great-grandmother's faces were not smiling with joy to see us. Their smiles had been replaced with a look I had never seen before, joylessness. When we arrived at my great-grand parent's home, the selfish child in me didn't want all those people around. I remember people everywhere, crying, singing, mumbling, and whispering; something was wrong. I had never before seen so many people in one place. They were hugging each other and my mother. I thought that they were hurting my mother and each other because the water faucet in all their eyes wouldn't stop. Little drops of water were falling on me as I stood beneath them. Some of them were also making strange animal noises. People's hands were everywhere waving in all different directions. I finally found my mother's hand that offered security to me and held on for dear life. I remember wishing I could get back in the car and go home.

As people continued to fill the room, I saw some of my cousins and we began to play, then we were told to sit down and be quiet by strangers, and were not allowed to go outside and play either. Also, we could not play with great-grandfather's sock monkey. The adults told us that if the monkey came out to play with us that it would create a fight. I didn't understand how just me playing with great-grandpa's monkey would cause a fight. Of course, I knew the other grand and great-grandchildren were there, but I was always the one who got to play with the monkey when I came to visit great-grandpa. Why was this time any different? I ran to the big bed that great-grandpa rode and tried hopping up on it so I could find him and the monkey even though I had been told that great-grandpa and the monkey were no longer there. Nothing was fun and I wanted to go home. I began to cry from frustration and became angry for not getting my way. A stranger picked me up trying to comfort me thinking I was upset about great-grandpa because she said, "It's okay, he is gone to be with the Lord." I looked up at this stranger and struggled to get out of her arms.

The next day my parents told my brother and me that we were going to a place called a funeral parlor. I knew it had to be fancy because mom had dressed us in our Sunday church clothes that we didn't like. When we had to wear our church clothes, we couldn't play or get dirty, just sit and pretend we were statuettes. What I remember about this first visit to this fancy place called a funeral parlor was that there were big, long black boxes in the biggest rooms I had ever seen. There were flowers that smelled, but not like the ones on grandma's farm or even the ones at home that were all around those big, long black boxes in those rooms. The flowers were so pretty, I had to have just one so I tried to pick a flower from one of the pots when a hand belonging to someone I had never seen before popped my delicate little fingers and then said, "Don't touch those flowers again." I don't know if it was the shock of being told no or getting my hand popped by a stranger that caused tears to form in my eyes. As her brazen voice penetrated the air I could see every pair of eyes in the room staring at me. I felt my mom slip her hand over mine as she led me away from the flowers as I was telling her, "I only wanted one of them mommy."

The people in the room kept going over to the long, black box looking into it and some even reached into the black box. This place was no more fun than at great-grandma's house. Then suddenly all the children were allowed to get up and walk around but we were warned that if we were caught running we had to sit back down. All the grand and great-grandchildren wanted to see what was in that big, long, black box that everyone was looking into. We made our way ever so slowly towards the black box and up to the steps in front of it. Since some of the women used the steps to see into the box, we felt that we could to. We played paper, scissors, rock to see who would be the first one to climb the steps and look into the box. The winner looked into the black box and then looked down at the rest of us, "Grandpa is in the box." We then took turns looking into the box to see great-grandpa who was asleep. After all of us children had took a turn looking into the black box we wondered where did they hide the rest of great-grandpa and why was he in his Sunday church clothes like us, and why did great-grandma put her face powder on great-grand pa. The tallest one of us reached inside of the black box to wake grandpa up. After the tallest cousin took hold of great-grandpa's hand, he turned to the rest of us and said, "Grandpa is so cold and his hand is heavy. He won't wake up!" We agreed that all of us together would try to help wake great-grandpa, so the shortest ones climbed onto the top step and the taller ones on the step behind them. As we stood on the steps in front of this long black box, we all started calling great-grandpa together to wake up. Just so happened that as we stood there shouting for grandpa to wake up his eyes opened and we yelled to the top of our breath with great joy, "Grandpa's awake!"

A woman walked over to the big, long, black box and looked into it. She let out this hissing sound and then fell directly to the floor at our feet. Another woman looked into the black box and she started screaming very loudly that made all of us children cover our ears. Nope, they couldn't complain about us being loud anymore.

The spot where we stood suddenly became crowded with people looking into the long, big, black box where grandpa still laid as he was waking up. Didn't they know that we had not finished our turn looking at grandpa? Didn't they know that we were the ones who had awakened great-grandpa from his rest, so it was only fair that we got to talk to him first? Just then, a large man dressed in black walked into the room and looked into the long black box and said, "Everyone, would you please leave the room for a few minutes please!" After what seemed like a very long time, at least to us children, they allowed us to go back into the room where we found great-grandpa asleep again.

Early the next day mom dressed us in black clothing. Then people began coming to the house and again were everywhere. As I sat in a chair I saw that everyone was dressed in the same color, black, how dare they dress in the same color as us. Mom rushed us to our feet, then into the car where we sat for hours. Mom explained that we were going to the church for great-grandpa's funeral and then to graveyard, new words I didn't understand. We were in a long line of cars going very slow and my brother and I kept asking are we there. I don't remember much after that, I slept through the rest.

The next strange bedfellow in the house is Cancer. When I first arrived to my client's home,

I learned that she had been in remission for the past few years but the cancer had returned. She no longer communicated with family and her only words were yes and no. The cancer had robbed her not only of her vocabulary but her thought processing also. Often she said no but the correct answer was yes. To tell the difference I relied upon her family members. The first day there, I gave her a shower, the last trip to the bathroom. The second day there she was too weak to walk. Several days later, we transferred her into a hospital bed. From there she accepted that her life was slipping away. As she, her mother, and I prayed the Rosary together, we all shared the reality that her death was near. Without a voice we watched her (my client) tears as they flowed from her eyes. Her tears were for:

- Tears of pain, as she would never get to watch her own child grow into adulthood
- Tears for the loneliness that she knew her husband and child would share in her absence

- Tears for the pain that her family would experience as they learn to cope with all the emotions of her death
- Tears of fear, for she knew that she had to trust in her faith, praying that it was real. The faith that says there is a God even though you never saw Him nor known Him as you have your own earthly father
- Tears of knowing that you have traveled your last road, smelled your last flower, tasted your last cup of coffee, and your last of everything on earth. Never again, to enjoy the things that she took for granted in the short time of life that she was on earth

Holy Mary Mother of God, pray for us sinners now and at the time of our death. Amen.

Then her mother's tears joined hers. Her mother later shared that her heart was broke and the tears were for the ones that she knew her daughter would never cry again.

As she began to slip into deaths tenure, her body started shutting down as her brain began swelling even more as the tumor had come back with a vengeance. Her family now embraced for death, as it was very near. I watched as they realized how cruel death was as it gripped their hearts in ways they had not expected, especially her father. I watched the pain and anger that was upon his face as he held the hands of his little girl on her death bed. I could only imagine his thoughts of helplessness of knowing he once held her and protected her as she grew into adulthood. Could the joy he had from knowing that she once relied uponhim to make everything good for her now be haunting him, as he could not stop her tumor from growing. Did he feel like he was letting her down because he couldn't fix this situation as his little girl lay in the shadow of death? I watched this big gentle giant tenderly hold his daughter's frail hands in his as he stared into her closed eyes. I wondered if he questioned the fairness of why this was happening to his little girl. I found myself sharing his pain as tears formed in my eyes. I wondered if I would be as reserved as this father if it was my little girl instead of his. This was certainly a road that I did not want to travel. I watched this father move aside as her husband entered the room and walked to his wife's bedside, then he kissed her head so softly and said, "I love you." I turned my back to them all as the tears flowed from my eyes while watching the new fallen snow out the window.

A FOREIGN WINTER

By: Donna Robbins

As I stood on the front porch
My mind went beyond what I was seeing
Accepting what I could not explain
I bowed as if I were Queen of this foreign land

The sun stood still to let the earth unfold
A mystery retold as the snow fell softly with hints of silver and gold
Dusting the very soul of this land

The sparkle
The glitter was amazing to see
It held me spellbound and breathless
As I imagined how pure and white this ground
was
The first time God stretched forth His mighty
hand

As diamonds sparkled on the ground in front
of me
Trees stood perfectly still with a glaze of
aloofness
The wind sent forth a might echo that captured
all those that ventured to and fro
A bird in the background sang like a choir of
angels announcing that it would soon be spring

So bold this foreign land was to the eye
But soft to the hand as it stung as fire
This foreign land exposed a calm and peaceful
event
As I stood watching all that ventured out into
this winter coat
That this place had placed on

Each snowflake danced, twisted, and fell
Then stood perfectly still
To rest in the sun with a joyous note
Of perfect stillness

The next day different family members and
friends stopped to say goodbye to this young
lady. I watched as each one tried to offer a part
of themselves to her immediate family hoping
to offset the hurt that was taking its toll. This
stranger, cancer that was in this house escorted
the life from this young lady's body as her very
young daughter played between her spread legs
on the bed with her husband holding her hand,
and her parents sitting on the other side of her
bed. Those of us that watched death take a
lovely young lady away from the cross that she
was given to bear on earth to meet Jesus, would
be changed forever.

This thing called death makes us angry at
ourselves and our society. Is death being dead?
Do we handle death differently by attaching
age to it? When someone young dies it grips

our hearts with a heaviness that questions God
more so than when an older person dies, why?

_____

_____

_____

_____

_____

If the person is elderly, why is it that we feel
that they have lived a good life? This makes
my soul weep. Where did man get the idea that
if you're sixty-ish, seventy-ish, eighty-ish, or
ninety-ish that a person or their family can face
death easier than anyone below the age of sixty?
When did this become so?

Genesis 6: 1-3
When men began to multiply on earth and
daughters were born to them, 2 the sons of
heaven saw how beautiful the daughters of
man were, and so they took for their wives as
many of them as they chose, 3 Then the Lord
said: "My spirit shall not remain in man forever,

since he is but flesh. His days shall comprise one hundred twenty years."

I believe it is harder not easier to face death when you are old. Just think, when you say that a person has lived a long full life do you realize that you are telling them that they have to leave their spouses, children, their loved ones, and everything that took a lifetime to accomplish behind. You are telling them that they do not get to live out their golden years after figuring out life and must leave all behind what they have accomplished. To me this is cruel even though I have seen those who are ready to go meet the Lord.

The Darkest Hour – Donna Robbins

Black, blackness, wind howling, rain pouring, waiting for death
The darkest hour, the longest hour, the loneliest moments, waiting
When you think the father has forsaken you

Despair, loss, hurt as you bear the stripes aimed
at your soul
You fear the eyes of the Father has passed you
by
Where do you find courage to look up to heaven
So alone
As you look around
At the faces that you are leaving behind
Despair for all
Who will face this darkest hour too
Knowing that He bore it for all of us
Unbelieving as they hear
Your soul cry to the Father,
Why have you forsaken me
The black, blackness, wind howling, pouring
rain, waiting death's sting
The darkest hour, the longest hour, the loneliest
moments, waiting
Blackness, raging wind, pouring rain
As death rips the breath from your lips
As you give into the darkest hour
Oh the soul
As it hurts from the thorns of life
As He carries us to meet the Father

Face to face
Hear Him shout from the darkness
All who are lost

LiveSirach 4: 28 Even to the death fight for truth,
and the LORD your God will battle for you.

CHAPTER 13

The End to the Beginning

My spiritual walk with the Lord began in
January of 1985. But first, I need to give you a
little history so that you can see why that day
was so special.

1 Corinthians 12:1-11

1 Now in regard to spiritual gifts, brothers, I do
not want you to be unaware. 2You know how,
when you were pagans, you were constantly
attracted and led away to mute idols. 3 Therefore,
I tell you that nobody speaking by the spirit of
God says, "Jesus be accursed." And no one can
say, "Jesus is Lord," except by the holy Spirit.
4 There are different kinds of spiritual gifts
but the same Spirit; there are different forms of
service but the same Lord; there are different
workings but the same God who produces all
of them in everyone. 7 To each individual the
manifestation of the Spirit is given for some

benefit. * To one is given through the Spirit the expression of wisdom; to another the expression of knowledge according to the same Spirit; to another faith by the same Spirit; to another gifts of healing by the one Spirit; 10 to another mighty deeds; to another prophecy; to another discernment of spirits; to another varieties of tongues; to another interpretation of tongues. 11 But one and the same Spirit produces all of these, distributing them individually to each person as he wishes.

Does time as a child of God season our spiritual gifts? I believe so because when I was first saved I was full of fire but not wisdom. I didn't see the danger of doing battle with the devil or his angels. It is best to describe a new born Christian kind of like this, young, dumb, and stupid. This is what I mean by this statement. I have often heard that God protects the old and the young; I feel that God also protects those who are still new in HIS kingdom and those who are unacquainted with spiritual matters. I know this to be true and you will too after I describe my first encounter with the spiritual world.

Shortly after I met John, who later became my husband, I changed jobs and started working for a different business. Shortly after I started this new job, a new manager was also appointed. After this new manager took over his duties, he began to remove the clutter from the store. Under the counter at the cash register he came across a Gideon Bible and he tossed it into a trash can, not so gently. I took the Gideon Bible out of the trash can and placed it on the counter. The manager picked up the Bible from the counter and threw it again into the trash can. I pulled it out of the trash can and placed it back on the counter. The manager for the third time threw the Gideon Bible into the trash can. As I reached into the trash can I looked him straight in the eye and said, "You do not throw away a Bible" with a firm voice as I pulled it out of the trash can. He looked at me and said, "If you want that Bible go put it in your car. IT WILL NOT remain in this store."

I took the Gideon Bible and put it in my car and I took it home.

Over the next several months, I began asking this new manager some questions regarding his faith, Satanism. I had never met a person who actually confessed that they worshiped Satan. Due to my eagerness to explore and ask questions he must have took this to mean that I wanted to become one of their flock, because Satan himself paid me a visit in person. I lived in a silver bullet camper in South Carolina; it was the month of August and was very hot on this particular night. I did not have air conditioning in the camper. Both doors were open to allow in some breeze. Suddenly a cloud of fog with a cold breeze rolled through the back door into the living room. I could smell something that was similar to burning hair combined with cigarette ashes. I truly don't know how to give a clear description of how it smelled; in retrospect could it have been sulfur. I could see the cloud of fog right in front of me that was accompanied by bloodcurdling laughter. Then a hideous voice spoke and kept repeatedly saying, "You will be with me tonight." I was so terrified. I remembered the Gideon Bible and could see it on the shelf under the TV stand where I had put it when I brought it home. I lunged forward, grabbed the Gideon Bible and clenched it to my chest. I began to pray, "Dear God I don't know you but I do not want to go to hell with him. Please don't leave me God." I prayed this repeatedly with the Bible cuddled to my chest till daylight.

Before John and I were married, John went into the hospital on the Air Force base for mono. After a week in the hospital the doctor would not discharged him unless someone could be with him for the first few days, so I let him stay with me until he could go back to his barracks. We had to make room for some of John's things in the silver bullet camper where I was living at the time. That's when we found a diamond ring and wedding band that mysteriously appeared in the bottom of a paper bag that fit me perfectly. I didn't know where the rings came from and had no idea how to track down whoever the original owner was. John took it as a sign from God and asked me to marry him on the spot. Before he went back to live in the barracks we were married.

When we got married, we used what little money we had as a down payment on a mobile home so that we would have a place to live. We bought our little mobile home shortly before Christmas of 1984 and moved in. When we got married, we couldn't afford to buy him a wedding ring due to buying our mobile home, but God provided.

In January of 1985 I had only been married about a month to my husband, John who was in the Air Force, when he was sent on his first temporary duty (TDY) to England for thirty days. I never put a connection with the number 30 that has come up numerous times in my life until I wrote this book; if I were a gambling woman I would bet on that number.

The day after John left for his TDY, I found a gold wedding band on a shelf beside the front door of our mobile home that we bought after we were wed. After John arrived in England, he called to let me know that he had arrived safely. I asked him then why he had bought a wedding band only to leave it at home. He informed me he had not bought a wedding band and that he had no idea of what I was referring to. See we both had put keys and other things on that shelf by the front door for about three weeks prior to this but neither one of us had ever seen the man's gold wedding band there. When John came home from his TDY, he tried on the wedding band, a perfect fit.

January 1985 I was saved. Yes, I mean saved as in born again Christian while John was on his first TDY in England. I was all alone in the small mobile home that we had bought. I picked up the Gideon Bible that I had taken from work and stared reading it. I flipped through it several times, as it lay on the floor in front of me. I got up off the floor and laid down on the couch. I closed my eyes. I felt like I was floating. I opened my eyes to make sure that I was still on the couch. I closed my eyes and I felt like I was floating again. So I opened my eyes again and I was in deed on the couch. The feeling was so intense that I questioned what was happening to me. I then figured that maybe I just needed a good nap. I closed my eyes and again I felt like I was floating. This time I decided to see what would happen next so I kept my eyes closed. I felt like my body completely left the couch when suddenly I saw a child running up a set of stairs that stretched as far as you could see in width and height. A light at the top of those stairs shown brighter than the sun it seemed. I sat up immediately and looked around the room. I got up off the couch and walked over to where the Gideon Bible lay on the floor. I sat down and started reading it again. I was flipping through the pages when a passage underlined in red caught my attention. I read it over and over and begin to cry. The tears left a stain on the pages of my Gideon Bible that remain there today. I got up off the floor, walked over to the couch and laid back down. When I closed my eyes, I began to float again. I honestly could not feel the couch underneath me. I saw the steps and the little child running up them and at the top of the stairs I could only see the outline of a chair that was made for a king beside a shadow of a man with a robe draped over him with outstretched arms to me surrounded by bright light. I realized then that it was Jesus as he stood there to greet me. Then the child disappeared from sight and I realized that the child was me. I knew that I was a child of the King and I was loved.

Hebrews 2:3-5

3 how shall we escape if we ignore so great a salvation? Announced originally through the Lord, it was confirmed for us by those who had heard. 4 God added his testimony by signs, wonders, various acts of power, and distribution of the gifts of the holy Spirit according to his will.

About four years after being saved John and I moved into a house we bought in a nearby town. Just about every day for over a month, this young man kept stopping to talk to us as we worked out in the front yard. He always bummed a cigarette from us and smoked it while talking to us. But this young man became bolder as he kept coming over. One evening we invited him in so that he wouldn't have to stand outside in the dark when he stopped by to ask if he could buy a pack of cigarettes from us. As he stood in the middle of our living room talking our youngest daughter suddenly came running out of her bedroom announcing, "A hand, a hand, a hand." As she made her announcement, she pointed up to the ceiling. The young man turned as white as a bed sheet and burst out the door, without his cigarettes. We stood still for several more minutes then went inside her bedroom where she continued to point and speak of the hand as she pointed up to the ceiling.

Several days later, this young man came walking down the sidewalk when he stopped in front of our house. There were steps coming from the sidewalk into the front yard leading to the front porch. This particular day as he stood above me on the sidewalk he started quoting scripture to prove a point he was trying to make. At this time in my life, my spiritual wisdom of the Bible was still growing as I struggled with reading God's word daily. But as God would have it, the verse this young man was quoting had been one I had just read; you guessed it, I called him out on it. He then tried using another passage from the Bible to back up the first one when God gave me the wisdom to call him out on that one too. As this young man and I stood there in a spiritual battle, my husband walked onto the front porch to see what was happening due to raised voices. As John started to open his mouth to confront this young man, God placed his hands on John's shoulders and made him sit on the bench by the front door with his mouth closed. Then God used me to do battle with this young man. John to this day says that he felt hands push him into a sitting position onto the bench and his tongue was silenced. I do not know what all I said that day but I knew then as well as now that I was not in control of my own body, words, or emotions. We never saw this young man again after this.

1st Corinthians 14: 20 Brothers, stop being childish in your thinking. In respect to evil be like infants, but in your thinking be mature.

After moving to New York, I attended a prayer service one night in our church. I felt an unusual coldness spreading across the room. I looked up when this shadow caught my attention as I looked into the three stained glass windows behind the church's altar. The three stain glass windows behind the altar from left to right each contained a figure, the first was Mary Mother of Jesus, the second window in the middle was Jesus the Son of God, and the figure in the third window was Joseph, Jesus' earthly father; the Holy family. But on this night, the figure that was in the middle window contained a dark figure, Satan himself. There were two pointed nubs on the top of his head and a black cloak draped around him that reminded me of Dracula. His stair was cold as ice as he surveyed all of us praying. I closed my eyes and opened them again; I didn't believe what I was seeing. When I opened my eyes he was still there staring at us praying. I closed my eyes again, I don't know why maybe it was because I didn't want to believe what I was seeing, but when I opened my eyes again, he was gone. After the prayer meeting was over I told my husband what I had seen, he just stared at me.

Job 2: 1-13

1 Once again the sons of God came to present themselves before the Lord, and Satan also came with them. 2 And the Lord said to Satan, "Whence do you come?" And Satan answered the Lord and said, "From roaming the earth and patrolling it." 3 And the Lord said to Satan, "Have you noticed my servant Job, and that there is no one on the earth like him, faultless and upright, fearing God and avoiding evil? He still holds fast to his innocence although you incited me against him to ruin him without cause." 4 And Satan answered the Lord and said, "Skin for skin! All that a man has will he

give for his life. 5 But now put forth your hand and touch his bone and his flesh, and surely he will blaspheme you to your face." 6 And the Lord said to Satan, "He is in your power; only spare his life." 7 So Satan went forth from the presence of the Lord and smote Job with severe boils from the soles of his feet to the crown of his head. 8 And he took a potsherd to scrape himself, as he sat among the ashes. 9 Then his wife said to him, "Are you still holding to your innocence? Curse God and die." 10 But he said to her, "Are even you going to speak as senseless women do? We accept good things from God; and should we not accept evil?" Through all this, Job said nothing sinful. 11 Now when three of Job's friends heard of all the misfortune that had come upon him, they set out each one from his own place: Eliphaz from Teman, Bildad the Shuh, and Zophar from Naamath. They met and journeyed together to give him sympathy and comfort. 12 But when, at a distance, they lifted up their eyes and did not recognize him, they began to weep aloud; they tore their cloaks and threw dust upon their heads. 13 Then they sat down upon the ground with him seven days and seven nights, but none of them spoke a word to him; for they saw how great was his suffering.

Satan continues to roam the earth even today searching out who he can make an example out of before God. This makes me wonder about the statement that I have heard before, "Why does God allow bad things to happen to good people?"

Revelation 3:19-21
19 Those whom I love, I reprove and chastise. Be earnest, therefore, and repent. 20 Behold, I stand at the door, and knock. If anyone hears my voice and opens the door, [then] I will enter his house and dine with him, and he with me. 21 I will give the victor the right to sit with me on my throne, as I myself first won the victory and sit with my Father on his throne.

I am glad that I am God's child.

CHILDREN

By Donna Robbins

You raise them
And then they are gone
Then you're forgotten
And all alone

Parents
They completed their job
And thought they were done
Then they find out
Their voices go unwanted
Leaving them more alone
Than before

Some get to say good bye
And others never do
But our Heavenly Father
Never forsakes us

I have never been comfortable with my gift of
discernment of spirits but I have come to accept

it. Over the years, God has revealed the presence of evil spiritual forces or influences while I worked in home health care, the nursing home, in my neighborhood, and in God's house to me. I have also learned that I cannot rely on my own understanding and judgment concerning these spirits. Through scripture I have learned that in order to understand this gift that I have to rely on the Holy Spirit through the word of God and that I must pray and constantly read God's Word, and keep my feet ready to go; the short version of this that I keep repeating to myself and family goes this way, prayed up, stayed up, and ready to go. God's word provides me with truth and understanding in order to do battle within the spiritual world. Without this knowledge from God's word, you cannot envision what could happen to me or you if we relied on our own intellectual abilities to do battle within the spiritual realm.

Acts 19:13-16
13 Then some itinerant Jewish exorcists tried to invoke the name of the Lord Jesus over those

with evil spirits, saying, "I adjure you by the Jesus whom Paul preaches." 14 When the seven sons of Sceva, a Jewish high priest, tried to do this, 15 the evil spirit said to them in reply, "Jesus I recognize, Paul I know, but who are you?" 16 The person with the evil spirit then sprang at them and subdued them all. He so overpowered them that they fled naked and wounded from that house.

When dealing with evil spirits it is unwise to allow your inward feelings to guide and direct you in spiritual warfare instead of allowing God's Holy Spirit to instruct you through the Scriptures. While working in home health care, this particular client was friendly when she met me at the door. She directed me to where I could put my paperwork and coat as we walked through the living room into the kitchen. She had suffered a heart attack and then had to have open heart surgery. I noticed as we went through her personal care in the bathroom that she was doing remarkable well. I then asked her what she wanted me to prepare her for breakfast but she declined saying that she had cereal earlier and didn't really care for anything to eat. But she then sat down at the kitchen table and in front of her was an open Bible. She began telling me about what was going on in her home. I don't know why she thought I could help but I listened as she began telling me of a spirit that lived upstairs. She stated that she use to sleep upstairs until one night she saw something in the hall; just the shadow frightened her so that she moved downstairs into a room off of her kitchen. She then proceeded to tell me that after moving downstairs that she awoke one morning to the bed bouncing, bouncing to the point that she almost fell off. She then described a conversation with someone from her church who gave her a prayer to pray. She took the piece of paper with the prayer written on it from her Bible. She asked if I would read it. She then asked if I knew anything about this prayer because it did not seem to be working with the spirit that she had in her home. As I took the paper, a cool wind blew into the kitchen. As I began reading the paper, I realized that it was from the Bible. I turned her Bible to Ephesians, Chapter 6 that described the armor of God.

Ephesians 6: 10-20 Battle against Evil.
10 Finally, draw your strength from the Lord and from his mighty power. 11 Put on the armor of God so that you may be able to stand firm against the tactics of the devil. 12 For our struggle is not with flesh and blood, but with the principalities, with the powers, with the world rulers of this present darkness, with the evil spirits in the heavens. 13 Therefore, put on the armor of God, that you may be able to resist on the evil day and, having done everything, to hold your ground. 14 So stand fast with your loins girded in truth, clothed with righteousness as a breastplate, 15 and your feet shod in readiness for the gospel of peace. 16 In all circumstances, hold faith as a shield, to quench all [the] flaming arrows of the evil one. 17 And take the helmet of salvation and the sword of the Spirit, which is the word of God. 18 With all prayer and supplication, pray at every opportunity in the Spirit. To that end, be

watchful with all perseverance and supplication for all the holy ones 19 and also for me, that speech may be given me to open my mouth, to make known with boldness the mystery of the gospel 20 for which I am an ambassador in chains, so that I may have the courage to speak as I must.

We sat for the next half hour deciphering what this passage meant and how she could apply it. With each question that she asked, I gave her answers and turned to the Holy Scripture for back up as I guided her through the steps that she would need. She wanted to find peace in her own home again. She was very receptive to the information that I gave her. As she and I entered the living room I picked up my coat and put it on, as I turned to say goodbye to my client, I came face to face with the spirit she had been describing to me that morning. This spirit seemed to consume this client's body; all I could see was the eyes and mouth of this spirit and how morally repulsive and frightening it was. I ran to the front door, opened it and never closed it behind me, got into to my car as fast as I could, drove off and never looked back. I knew that I was not stayed up, prayed up, ready to go, nor did I have my whole armor of God polished even though I had just spent the last half hour reviewing it for my client. There comes a time when you understand who you are, compared to who you think you are. This was one of those times when I was caught with my spirituality pulled down to the floor. I knew though that I had to get my spiritual life in order because one day I might have to go back to this client's home.

The next story describes how a friend learned to cope after a devastating accident as a young man. JPJ and I became friends in the midst of a storm that at times exhausted our moral compasses as we shared our Christian beliefs while witnessing the morality of our individual faiths. The following is his story. There are things that I do not agree with but to give true insight to his story they have to be added as he wished them to be known concerning his transformation on the road that he traveled to become a child of God.

JPJ believes that our personalities are formed within the human living environment during the early years of life and that parents are responsible to guide the good and bad influences.

Jeremiah1:4-5
4 The word of the LORD came to me thus: 5 Before I formed you in the womb I knew you, before you were born I dedicated you, a prophet to the nations I appointed you.

JPJ also believes that parents and the environment are reinforcements that determine our psychic patterns that develop our personality. I personally believe that our personality is given to us when God sanctified us before we were born in His image. I also believe that temptation started in the Garden of Eden and came from Satan that caused us to neglect our perfect nature and follow the desires that he manifested to Adam and Eve that caused human beings to commit sin that changed their relationship with God as described in the Book of Genesis in the Bible.

JPJ believes that the narcissistic personality comes into play when one or both parents demonstrate full acceptance and admiration that breeds an over confident personality. Experts' use the Diagnostic and Statistical Manual of Mental Disorders (DSM-5), published by the American Psychiatric Association to diagnose human beings, whereas God's word addresses self-esteem many times.

JPJ feels that the dependent and borderline personality is a result of neglect by one parent but accepted by the other parent, causing the child to always seek emotional dependency in life, accepts them. This results in those personalities becoming a loyal helper or becomes a physical personality that wants control of situations. And last is the histrionic personality disorder where one parent was extremely close to the child but the other parent neglected the child causing social dilemmas.

The views described here are JPJ's as related to his many years as a counselor and studying psychology. He stated that these personalities go through life forming relationships, marriage, and divorce while seeking someone that will love them for who they are and stay with them. He also stated that if they can maintain a good marriage and have children that they can be healthy and productive in society. But that even as the person ages, the career they pursue depends on how much money they can make. I do agree with him that most human beings choose a career not suited for them due to the money aspect.

JPJ at the age of 17 encountered an accident that left him paralyzed and restricted to a wheelchair for the rest of his life. This accident changed his perspective regarding his future. This is his story.

On May 26, 1970, I remember diving into the cold clear water of Lake Tahoe and hit a rock. It felt like a sledgehammer hit my head. Then

I saw my blood. I was not able to feel my body as I became aware that I couldn't move my legs. I knew that I was going to drown. As I slipped under the water, I began to suffocate. I remember wishing that I would go back up to the surface like I use to do at the city pool after holding my breath, gasping for air as I reached the surface. But this time I couldn't reach the top. The horror set in. I WAS GOING TO DIE AND THERE WAS NOTHING, I MEAN NOTHINGTHAT I COULD DO ABOUT IT. Images of my life flashed through my mind in seconds. I was drowning. I called out to GOD in telepathic message. I was telling Him that I didn't want to die. I do believe had I not struggled with my will to live that day, I would have died. These memories remain with me every moment of every day. When the will to live no longer exists or gives up, the person or living soul dies. It is not a matter of sickness, injury, or disease, but the desire TO LIVE. Without the desire to live, the soul commits suicide. The soul is very angry at itself and others that have hurt it. As a result it commits self-murder. Do you know how hard it is for someone to take their life? It takes tremendous pride and emotional pain known as grief to do it. Grief is a life process by which we sort out our mistakes and hope to learn from them.

I took my last breath and died while sinking to the bottom of Lake Tahoe. My human spirit was in a pure black void. Upon entering this void, I no longer experienced any physical pain or discomfort, suspended as I waited to return to my body. I had no idea of what my fate would be. Then I remembered waking up in great pain. A nurse told me that I was in intensive care at the hospital, that I had injured myself.

I struggled physically and mentally the next five years to adjust to the life of a paraplegic in a wheelchair, which left me angry as I confronted this bad hand that God had dealt me. The beginning of my college years was the worst as I dealt with lack of companionship and isolation. This was a very lonely time for me, but in the process of working through my pain and loneness, I began a search for God. The result, I became a Christian in my junior year of college through Campus Crusade for Christ. Becoming a Christian was the greatest thing that happened to me but I continued to wonder what happened to me in that black void. I read articles that described it as a near death experience. I read a few books that described what happened as the tunnel of death that was like a cornucopia and that I had been in the small end of the tunnel that was the blackness I experienced.

Some years later after college I became a Drug and Alcohol Abuse Counselor. In this line of work I met a few people that had experienced a near death experience similar to mine. This only gnawed away at me for not having the answers that I was looking for. I was still growing deeper in my Christian walk as I continued seeking God more and more. Then I decided I needed to seek Jesus more because my life became like a nomad, I wasn't able to become stable in any one place. Then I left to go live in Hawaii. It was there that I experienced the cross of Jesus and surrendered my life to Christ. I wanted a good Christian woman and a family. As I strived to commit my life completely to Jesus Christ, I gained inner peace. I came back from Hawaii in 1981 broke. I planned to remain single for at least two years.

When you least expect it you meet the right person. I met my wife, my soul mate, and fell in love. We were married after three months. I told her that she didn't have to worry about birth control since I had a low sperm count. It was not Jesus' plan for us not to have children because two years after we were married she became pregnant with our first child and then again with our second son. As I continued to make a deeper commit to Christ, the better my life got.

Shortly after this, I started my private practice in drug and alcohol abuse counseling for a period of five years. After I ended my practice, I moved back to Canada and started adjusting to my life as a husband and father. Then I became ill with chronic osteomyelitis, an infection in the bone and bone marrow with necrosis because of my accident. I underwent surgery for this condition but even to this day I am still fighting it.

In the beginning of my diagnosis of osteo-myelitis, each day brought back my diving accident. I began to read more and more about my condition wondering if and when I would die. I thought that I was prepared for death since I had previously had an encounter with it in 1970, but the fact is, I am never prepared for death.

My Christianity gave me the greatest comfort. I would read my Bible but that gnawing feeling started at me again, what would happen to me if I died. I knew that I would be with Jesus but it still gnawed at me. I went often to the library and began to search. I became sidetracked and started studying about reincarnation. I decided to write a novel but I couldn't get it done. So a friend told me to buy a note book and write down every thought in it, so I did. In the process, I bought a thesaurus to help build words. Then I found a book in the library written in 1855 about transmigration, where one body passes after death into a soul. I then began to think about Dennis Rader known as the BTK killer, which stands for "Bind, Torture, Kill" that was his infamous signature. What is going to happen to him or the world if he transmigrates into another soul? Would he then grow up, commit suicide, and repeat again other means of suffering and death until he pays for the victims?

Eccl. 9:5-6.
5 For the living know that they are to die, but the dead no longer know anything. There is no further recompense for them, because all memory of them is lost. 6 For them, love and hatred and rivalry have long since perished. They will never again have part in anything that is done under the sun.

Then a fifty year old man lives out the most of his life with no criminal record walks into a store and kills two employees. One of the men that died was only 37 and was about to celebrated his 11th wedding anniversary that left two children fatherless. What happens to these killers? Do they go to hell? What about the victims of hurricane Katrina? People die every hour of the day. Are they sent back to be birthed again and grow up to pay for their karma debt. Karma retribution eventually becomes restitution maybe for Dennis Rader and others if they become a born again Christian.

Luke 16:19–31

19 There was a rich man who dressed in purple garments and fine linen and dined sumptuously each day. 20 And lying at his door was a poor man named Lazarus, covered with sores, 21 who would gladly have eaten his fill of the scraps that fell from the rich man's table. Dogs even used to come and lick his sores. 22 When the poor man died, he was carried away by angels to the bosom of Abraham. The rich man also died and was buried, 23 and from the netherworld, where he was in torment, he raised his eyes and saw Abraham far off and Lazarus at his side, 24 And he cried out, 'Father Abraham, have pity

on me. Send Lazarus to dip the tip of his finger in water and cool my tongue, for I am suffering torment in these flames.' 25 Abraham replied, 'My child, remember that you received what was good during your lifetime while Lazarus likewise received what was bad; but now he is comforted here, whereas you are tormented. 26 Moreover, between us and you a great chasm is established to prevent anyone from crossing who might wish to go from our side to yours or from your side to ours.' 27 He said, 'Then I beg you, father, send him to my father's house, 28 for I have five brothers, so that he may warn them, lest they too come to this place of torment.' 29 But Abraham replied, 'They have Mosses and the prophets. Let them listen to them.' 30 He said, 'Oh no, father Abraham, but if someone from the dead goes to them, they will repent,' 31 'Then Abraham said, 'If they will not listen to Moses and the prophets, neither will they be persuaded if someone should rise from the dead.'

This accident is the hardest thing I have had to encounter. The devastation was excruciating to my body and my ego (will) since I am a borderline personality. This left great anger in me, which I have used and still use to this day to do good. It has kept me alive and turned me into a fighter until God comes to take me home.

Each of us has a cross to bear. December 2000 I had an accident at work that stopped my career as a home health care aide that became my cross. In the moment of a second I quickly learned how some of my patients felt after they realized that their lives had changed forever. The last fifteen years I have lived with chronic pain from injury to my spine. There are a few things that I will mention that I have learned from this accident. One is humbleness before God. There is a song called God on the Mountain that I have heard sung by different people, which has gotten me through many a painful day. The words to the chorus of this song go like this:

[Chorus]
For the God on the mountain is still God in the valley

When things go wrong, He'll make them right
And the God of the good times is still God of
the bad times
And the God of the day is still God of the night,
(which is my favorite line.)

There was one point after my accident that pain
consumed all of me and I really thought the only
way out was death, so I walked down to the park
on our street with a bottle of pills. I don't know
how long I had been sitting on the bench in the
park staring at the bottle of pills in my hands.
As I took off the cap and poured the pills into
my hand, I heard two voices that sounded like
angels. I looked up and it was my two beautiful
daughters running towards me screaming don't
do it, don't do it. As they reached out and took
the pills out of my hands they told me how
important I was too them and that they didn't
want me to die. I don't know how they knew
because I had not told anyone what I was about
to do. I put the pills back in the bottle and we
walked home together. We never spoke of this
again. Shortly after this, my pain reached a new

record of unbearable. In the early hours of the morning, I mentally did not see how I could bear the pain any longer. I got down on my knees that would not bend and prayed for Jesus to come take me home. Instead, he came and sat down on the edge of my bed and held my head in his lap. I sobbed until I fell asleep while Jesus stroked my hair. I awoke at dawn and realized that I was still on my knees, but for the first time in a long time, the pain was bearable. I lingered there on my knees with my head on the bed remembering how it felt when Jesus comforted me through this very difficult night. Since I was still here and He did not take me from this earth as I had asked I raised myself up from the floor and have managed to walk and sing every day since then. Today I still sing this song, God on the Mountain as I overcome daily my struggles with pain that sometimes rob me of enjoying life. I will as long as I live cling to that last line of the song, "And the God of the day is still God of the night." I realize that my Savior is always here for me, even in my darkest hours, even when I want to quit.

Luke 6:46-49

46 "Why do you call me 'Lord, Lord,' but not do what I command? 47 I will show you what someone is like who comes to me, listens to my words, and acts on them. 48 That one is like a person building a house, who dug deeply, and laid the foundation on rock; and when the flood came, the river burst against that house but could not shake it because it had been well built. 49 But the one who listens and does not act is like a person who built a house on the ground without a foundation. When the river burst against it, it collapsed at once and was completely destroyed."

DON'T QUIT

By: Donna Robbins

Upon a cold winters day
My heart beats to the rhythm of the chilly wing

And on a summer's night
My heart melts

As I try to find my place
.... either way ....
A joy of new direction rushes forth

Will my heart run the race
Will I cross the finish line

I can't say
But today
I learned to pray

Master
Help me do something just for you
Give me strength to overcome the battles
That pulls me down
Lift my head high again
So I can see

I just don't quit
Till you come to set me free

Do you know Jesus? If not I encourage you
to ask someone or even look me up. If you do

then I encourage you to share our Jesus with someone before it is too late for them.

Who Are You?

Donna: Are you ready for bed Sweetie?

Mrs. Sweetie: Who are you?

Donna: I am Donna.

Mrs. Sweetie: Who are you?

Donna: Who do you think I am?

Mrs. Sweetie: Donna.

Donna: That's right, I'm Donna.

Mrs. Sweetie: I love you Donna.

Donna: I love you too Mrs. Sweetie.

Mrs. Sweetie: You call me Mrs. Sweetie, have I always been sweet?

Donna: Yes, you have always been sweet.

Mrs. Sweetie: Are we kidding each other?

Donna: No, we are not kidding each other.

Mrs. Sweetie: Are you my sister?

Donna: No, I am not your sister.

Mrs. Sweetie: Who are you then?

Donna: I'm your aide, Donna.

Mrs. Sweetie: I love you Donna.

Donna: I love you too Mrs. Sweetie.

Mrs. Sweetie: Who am I?

Donna: You are Mrs. Sweetie.

Mrs. Sweetie: I am?

Donna: Yes you are.

Mrs. Sweetie: Where is my father?

Donna: He has been deceased for many, many years. Mrs. Sweetie you are 94 years old.

Mrs. Sweetie: I am? I am really 94 years old?

Donna: Yes Mrs. Sweetie, you're really 94 years old.

Mrs. Sweetie: Who are you?

Donna: Who do you think I am?

Mrs. Sweetie: Donna.

Donna: That's right, I'm Donna.

Mrs. Sweetie: I can't talk, I have teeth.

Donna: You're doing a good job with them.

Mrs. Sweetie: No I am not.

Donna: Okay, we will take your teeth out as soon as you get to the bathroom to get ready for bed.

Mrs. Sweetie: Who are you?

Donna: Who do you think I am?

Mrs. Sweetie: Donna.

Donna: Yes that's right, I am Donna.

Donna Robbins

Mrs. Sweetie: I love you Donna.

Donna: I love you too Mrs. Sweetie. It is time to go to bed.

Mrs. Sweetie: No! I want to stay in my chair.

Donna: Mrs. Sweetie, it is ten thirty at night, don't you want to lie down?

Mrs. Sweetie: Who are you?

Donna: Who do you think I am?

Mrs. Sweetie: Donna.

Donna: Yes that's right. How about let's get you in bed where you can stretch out and rest?

Mrs. Sweetie: Yes I want to go to bed now. Who are you?

Printed in the United States
By Bookmasters